P9-BZP-051

Tears of Bliss:

A Guru-Disciple Mystery

A Spiritual Autobiography

By Narvada Puri
Disciple of Baba Santosh Puri
Of Sri Panch Dasnam Juna Akhara

Published by Santosh Puri Ashram
Printing & distribution by Cinnamonteal Print and
Publishing

Tears of Bliss: A Guru-Disciple Mystery
Copyright © 2009 Santosh Puri Ashram.
All rights reserved.

No part of this book may be reproduced, translated,
transliterated, or transmitted in any form or by any
means, whether electrical, mechanical, or digital
including photocopying, recording, or any information
storage and retrieval system, without the permission
in writing of the copyright holder.

Cover Design, artwork, and photo pages layout by
Xavier Froment.
Typed and edited by Dharmi (Darcy) Cunningham.
Photographs are from our albums and files, donated
by many friends and disciples.

Printed at Cinnamonteal Print and Publishing
in Goa, India.

ISBN : 978-81-907296-5-9

CONTENTS

EDITOR'S NOTE

<u>Tears of Bliss</u> is written in Mataji's (Narvada Puri) voice. As I read it for the first time, and even the twentieth, I hear her voice speaking, telling the story and the teachings woven within these pages. That voice still has a bit of German accent, after all these years. With the grace of artistic license, we have used a voice and structure reflecting simultaneously the non-native English speaker and the eloquence of a poet, as long as this did not create confusion for the reader. Nuances in words and grammar often reflect other-worldly events and relationships. So read this with your heart open and let the divine story flow over you!

Many words and chants are left in Sanskrit and Hindi because no single English word, or even phrase, can really capture the meaning of the holy language of Sanskrit. We have footnoted these words and phrases on the page they first appear; those words which reoccur are also listed in the glossary in the back of the book.

I bow in gratitude and love to Mataji and Babaji, whose Divine Grace has resulted in the beauty of this work; any typos or errors are mine.

OM Namo Narayan (I bow to the Divine in all)
Dharmi (Darcy) Cunningham

Dedication and Acknowledgements

Inexpressible devotion to the lotus feet of your root Guru, Sri Santosh Puri Baba, Avadhut, whose motherly hand introduced your ignorant soul into a heavenly bliss of sat-chit-ananda, manifested in the form of all that is, including yourself.
His guiding light removed your blindness to see that nothing else other than eternal consciousness is shining its infinity through all and a blessed medium.

The Guru's grace brought you to a lifelong surrender to Lord Ganesha, Sada Shiv, and the Universal Mother to place your budding awakening into a community of Saints and exalted beings.

Worldly thanksgiving go to all the many loving brothers and sisters of the soul who supported and encouraged your written expression by experiencing a familiarity of oneness with their own inner quest.

A special deep affinity has to reach Dharmi (Darcy Cunningham) whose devoted sacrifice of months and nights edited the book to what it is now.

Useful assistance was received from Xavier Froment, from France, who designed the cover and the photo outlay.

Not to forget Richie Joshua Windus from America, who gave the first financial support to settle a vision of the heart into the press of points and headlines.

Love and austerity to live your true nature!
OM Namo Shivaya

PREFACE

Holy scriptures need no introduction, let alone any comments. What ignorance in accepting the impossible task of writing this preface! Yet, the reading provides humble faith in the unavoidable.

This autobiography is a wonderful, yet down to earth story of a western woman finding liberation at the feet of an Indian Guru, Baba Santosh Puri. The sweet discovery of the one promised in a dream is followed by harsh austerities embraced with rare devotion. The young woman has become the teacher's child, Narvada. Together they wield starvation of body and mind as the sword to kill the one who never lived. On a small river island near the holy city of Haridwar, ten years begin and end with Ganga, Baba, cow service, love, acceptance and the never-ending bliss of Shiv Shiv Shiv.

Yet, upon the brink of death, karma reveals her path to liberation passing through family life, as the ultimate sacrifice of a renunciate. Through the love of her God incarnated, Narvada gives birth to three blessed children in order to become a Mataji (mother) to the universe. Renunciation is thus brought to a deeper level, yet the illusion of a liberation coming from somewhere remains.

Finally, as the children turn into young adults, Babaji performs the final ritual to reveal the ultimate Guru-disciple mystery. Voluntarily leaving his body behind, he withdraws to eternity that which has been the center of Narvada's devotion for about three decades. Yet, the love remains and now has no choice left but to find its true source. Which it does.

From the first sentences of this book it is clear that explanation is not Mataji's objective. Facts are simply written down directly from the heart. Often not even short sentences are required. No need for objectivity, justification, reflection after the fact. Events, thoughts, and feelings are narrated as they manifested in their own now. Acceptance is engrained in the humble poetry.

While utterly personal, this book treats a number of universal questions. Any spiritual seeker will find answers here that go way beyond the conceptual. Their clarity shines through the words, as truth originating from direct experience. They need no academic analysis. Neither is it up to this preface to reveal them.

Yet, the questions answered are worth considering. Having some true experience with yoga, means having some experience with the bliss of the divine inside. That is the easy part, awaiting all that are willing to make a little effort. But the main question remains: how to see it with open eyes? How to hold it in the palm of one's hand? How to turn deceitful

Maya into divine Lila? How to jump from ever-vulnerable experience to eternal reality? How to accept freedom?

Some less final but still essential pieces of the spiritual puzzle are also put into place. How can anger represent the most loving sacrifice of the Guru? Where to surrender what? Why never ask why? When must even renunciation be renounced? How to see the perfect in the perfect? How to stop getting caught in all these questions of duality?

I do like to reveal one golden drop stolen from this ocean of wisdom: "Contentment (Santosh) is self-sufficiency". May all who have ears, hear and lay their minds at rest near the feet of this mother.

Blessed is the reader of these tears of bliss. Blessed is the one who shed them. Blessed is the source of all.

Om Namo Narayan,

Peter Marchand
Ghent, Belgium

Prologue: Three Hymns to the Guru[1]

The taste of something God-like for the Real,
Full plain pages
Where to start?
Babaji's Memorial Darshan[2]
Is so complete in itself:
Impossible to take out some part
Of His heavenly incarnation.
Visions everywhere of His immense love and care
when I, His newborn child,
Had been most in need of it.
When I try to write "Him" down,
The "He" escapes, not to be grasped and put into words,
Dissolving in the Infinite.
Follow Him
And dissolve yourself.

---

[1] One who leads from darkness to light, a realized/liberated being.

[2] Sight; vision of the divine, of Truth; being in the presence of a realized being.

One
Shri Guruve Namah
OM Guruji
Please give me the bliss to write down Your
Greatness,
To tell and manifest how much my heart had loved
You,
To be able to realize in all Your worldly form
A glimpse of the Divine.

OM Guruji
Everything became a lesson to teach me that the
Absolute is pervading in You and in all.

Where to start ... where to finish.
Still waiting for the creative moment to plant the holy
tree in memory of Guruji's shy incarnation.
A tree to grow out of devotion,
To blossom from the enthusiasm of Divine teaching,
To bear fruit in the hearts of some followers,
To serve on the Path to the end of suffering.

Still waiting
To listen to Krishna's flute.
To inspire, to follow, to write down, to sing,
To forget day and night, hunger and thirst.

Om Guruji
Apologizing in ignorance – with tears –
What is there to excuse,

What to forgive,
What has been missed
And left unfulfilled?

In reality there is no veil, no Maya[3], even no
ignorance,
Only and forever Your smiling, loving presence,
In friend's form according to my childish vision.

A humble approach
To catch a part of the Divine
And manifest it as a proof.

---

[3] Illusion: everything of the manifest world is illusion in Vedic
philosophy. Maya is the limited, purely physical and mental
reality in which our everyday consciousness has become
entangled, a veiling of the true, unitary Self.

Two
OM
Guruji
Deoji
Dattaji
Swamiji
Paramatmaji[4]
OM Namo Narayan

From where I know the far away,
All the unseen that was never unfolded in front,
All hints to lead the way up to the unknown.
You are all. That's what I know.
But how to grasp You in this game
As my eyes are covered:
Losing is winning –
And winning is losing.
Sit still in the void, the light is waiting.
OM Babaji[5].
Another time again,
Begging for a visible proof of my surrender,
Desire for devotion in the form of austerity retreat.
And again begging for an endless meditation.
But can I fulfill more than I am able to do?
Still another day, another day –
When will come the other day,
To pour out and down on paper
The beautiful memorials

---

[4] Mantras to surrender to the Guru.
[5] Term of affection for a holy man.

Of Babaji, the divine heritage?
Still what can I do?
It is all for Him to let it happen.
Knowing everything,
Still unable
To reach for the treasure next door,
Taking the darkness for the beginning of light.

Back in the home of the soul,
Cared for and forever:
OM Namah Shivaya[6] – the mantras are the key, the
tool.
The wonder of Babaji's beauty will never stop.
He – the One from above –
Bestowed with divine qualities,
Incarnated for the Truth.
Fight for It,
Suffer for Its defeat.
Everywhere inertia, laziness, carelessness, weakness.
Why? How long do we play the part?
How long before we can see clearly?
The Divine vanishes,
Lifts up, and dissolves in its origin;
Lost forever in its visible form,
To gain again through worship.

So true,
There has never been a time
When Babaji hasn't been or will not be,

---

[6] Mantra meaning Salutations to Shiva, the Formless One.

Because He and I and the Universe are interwoven,
Inseparable through the cause of karma[7],
Always remembered and perceived through bhakti[8],
Taken by His hand of faith and surrender,
Abandoned to fall only into His arms again.
What an endless game!

Babaji's smile is embracing,
Giving courage and new life,
One only wonders
Why we are not leaving everything
To remain with this smile.
How shameful to abandon His presence,
So rare to realize, for what nonsense, all in all.
All knowing deep inside
Still going away.
Babaji's first and only lesson:
Shiv Shiv Shiv Shiv Shiv.
May I be able to live to it,
Now after times of "knowledge,"
Waiting for Grace to overcome my weakness
Another iron will:
Mumuksha[9]

---

[7] Law of cause and effect, past actions and lives have their
consequences in the future.
[8] Devotion.
[9] The burning desire for liberation.

Three
Babaji –
Part of myself
And still never understood.
So clear the visible
Or something more still:
This is that to which I bow.
OM Guruji.

Guruji-Babaji
Had been in front
Visible, touchable, to be spoken to, even to be
played with,
But by manifesting the Divine,
The Divine became bound to the form,
Therefore no more to be realized.
We cannot look for the Divine in the form –
Therefore we miss it.
Only from inside,
By grace or humble sadhana[10],
We become able to project the spirit into the form.
We find now what has already been there:
Not the Supreme Spirit in the form, but the form as
the form of the Supreme.

OM Guruji.
Always looking.
Praying for something that You had presented
already by Your Divine touch.

---

[10] Spiritual practices.

Oh ignorant Soul!
Always there, but blinded through the form.
OM Guruji.
OM Shiv Shiv Shiv Shiv.
Finally questioning and searching has come to its
end.
OM Shiv Shiv Shiv.
What follows is an abundance of peace, faith, and
strength.
The source of suffering is the inability to consider the
variety of things
Buried underneath,
No space left to breathe,
Too overloaded to see anything at all.
Now how easy – what simple beauty
Brahman – the one without another –
All is the One – the One is everything.
The riddle is solved,
No labyrinth to conquer
To find the solutions.
OM Shiva OM.

Part One: Dawn

ONE

As It All Began

Born into ignorance
As everybody, everything,
Not too good, not too bad,
Enjoying the predicted happiness,
Too insubstantial to last forever.
A crocodile of Truth starts awakening
To make the unavoidable feel
Its deluding presence.
The ground of Illusion has to be dug up
Through the contact with suffering:
Life's purifying teaching.

Childhood tears
Calls into the lonely nights of despair:
No hope, no courage
No chance of life to be felt.
Not even a slight imagination of the all-pervading
Consciousness
Floating, smiling, compassionate,
All over and around.

The bounty of miseries and cries,
The ever-unfulfilled,
The ever-watchful witness.
Time will come

Rays of light and Knowledge
Will pierce the small walls of ignorance,
Searching to land in a crying soul.
One night
Its light found your little childish being
In a far away desert of illusion (Germany).
Your tears dried up,
The sentimental pain forgotten.
You looked into the darkness.
All of a sudden
You know there is an Unknown to cling to
And to follow and follow.
Drawn into a universe of alien laws and beauty,
No vision!
Not even a sun can fix its reflection on mud and
misery.
Not knowing, not learning
But something incredibly powerful and universal
Had been there and will be there forever.
The growth of the lotus will start its struggle from
the mud to the light;
The blind one's constant crash against the wall;
Even the blind in time will find a hole to escape.
Nature of karma
Is pushing you through the desert,
Constantly increasing the thirst for the Immortal
water.
Your tears cannot make you drink,
And so time passes.
No uplifting by yourself;
Grace has to plant the signs you are going to meet.

The compassionate mother of destiny will teach you
to stand up and walk by yourself.

A Dream
A long white beard,
Waving,
The eyes seeing beyond the world,
Far behind the clouds.
The head an aura of light
The inexpressible peace of the seer, the knower, the
Light on the Path,
The end of the journey of confusion.

Twelve years before the meeting of the Guru,
This had been the vision of a twelve-year old girl
Dreaming of life's fulfillment.
India!!
Silk and spices,
Beauty, charm, elephants, the land of Siddhartha,
the Buddha,
Teaching the Truth in the Garden of Wisdom.
The solution can be found.
One day surely you will go.
The longing of the Soul remains,
The call for purity, Truth, and recognition.
The forces of illusion
Work hard to cover or to let forget.
The play of illusion builds its web.
The more you look for Truth,
The deeper you get involved in ignorance.

Innocent, searching for happiness,
But the sports of enjoyment increase to blood your
karma.
The fun goes on,
A risky dance on tears of desperation.
Had that been the expectation of the Soul?
Surely no friend in truth.
Destiny watches and waits and counts.
When the measure is full,
Time will throw you out of the net of trouble and
Place you on the Path.

To India
Around the auspicious 1970's, flashes of lightening
had been working all over the West to wake up the
children to leave their luxurious homes and go
barefoot on the road to India.
No more false predictions, nothing but Truth, Peace,
and Love for existence.
No sacrifice is too high.
The first renouncement of family, friends, profession,
country, cars, and cakes.
One bag, one blanket, one book, one flute, and, by
hitchhiking, to India!
Determination does not need an address;
You just follow the happy response in your heart.
On the way, the normal things of good and bad.
Not everything has lost its importance and influence,
just because of the goal you are aiming at.
India: the dream, the home, the chance, the end of
the journey!

You hear somebody saying, "I will go up along the
Ganga. There are Saints meditating in the cold, and
taking baths in the Ganga at three in the morning."
Sounds of a new good world.
You don't know why.
When you meet, you will recognize.

Delhi!
You have arrived.
Where is India, the Guru? Which direction: Goa,
Pondicherry, Banares?
Still hopeful for the solution to come,
Holding the balance,
Among broken freaks who search for imaginary
happiness.
One does not go by oneself in India:
You are led softly by the hand.
By whom you don't know,
No words to ask.

TWO

Pilgrimages to Fulfill Your Wishes

Vision of Shiva
Holy waters, holy places, holy people,
Can give you liberation in one moment.
It is possible!
Commonly called a "miracle:"
To remove the veil of ignorance,
To clear impurities stored up for generations.

Arrival in Banares[11] and the next day you got
enlightened!
Not forever, but enough to change life and work until
eternity to regain and establish the bliss.
In one minute a vision of Lord Shiva?
How is that possible?
An unimportant hippie, freaky and stupid and
impure, is embraced by the Lord Himself, engraving
His name, Shiv, forever into the heart!
No Knowledge of Brahman, the Vedas, the rituals,
the austerities.
Throwing away the crutches and the glasses,
No longer lame, no longer blind, you have
understood without being taught!

---

[11] Holy city of Lord Shiva.

"Come child of God,
Become a part of the divine celebration!"
The virtuous, the disciplined will reach the Supreme
Through endeavors of lifetimes.
When confusion, naughtiness, and craziness are in
dominance,
Then only the radical can work and help.
If God wants you to be saved:
The shock, the stick, or the drug,
One sparkle –
And the whole garbage burns to ashes.

The Shiva temple by the roadside solved the search
for the right place.
You just came back home,
You go straight up to the holy shrine.
The doors are still closed.
You don't ask who is inside.
You sit by the wall and your heart starts singing,
Flying high, knocking at the paradise unknown.
No question,
Your innocence is back,
You don't mind winning the prize.
The time was right,
The light could be recognized.
Shiv!
Your only real nature is
Everywhere at all sides – below, above, all around:
The seer and the experience have merged into one.
What immense peace has touched your heart all of a
sudden?

The last longings are gone,
The names have left,
Fulfilled their duty.
A medium towards the final peace of existence:
Shiva!
The peace of the mantra[12],
Not the mantra itself:
Golden light,
Millions of celestial faces
Melting into the one light:
Shiv, All is Shiv
Shiva – only Shiv –
A glimpse of the Supreme:
Enough to transcend the puzzle of the Universe
And give it the golden touch of Truth.
There is a way out!
God passed by –
The eternal smile of hope goes on.
Now Shiva has become everything and everywhere.
You can touch Him in the wall, love Him in the wind,
listen to Him in the drums of the snake tamers.
You can get up without losing Him.
You know now with whom you are dancing,
For whom you carried the flowers every day.
The temple doors are still closed.
Shiva is surely inside, as He is outside.
Whisper by the door.
Let your stubborn heart press Him: "If you don't

---

[12] A series of seed sounds, syllables whose meaning is beyond
the "word," leads one to the Reality itself. Repeated for
meditation and chanting or for some specific effect.

open, I will put the garland around the door handle
and worship the door as your Divinity!"
And look!
The garland is thrown back around your neck.
The play can start.
The garland flows to and fro.
Highest ecstasy:
Shiva is playing with His child who dares to play
back.
Hide and seek around the temple and look! The
temple door is now open.
The Shiva lingam[13] high and black
With the white tripund[14], the mark of His trinity.
Manifested Truth!
The playmate bows down to the knees.
The first flow of tears in recognition:
Shiva, the great Omniscient.
Endless moments of silence and adoration.
"Go my child and find my form!"
No knowledge of anything,
Only the reaction of the leaf in the morning wind, by
divine chance falling into the arms of the Lord.
The eternally pure is changing into movement,
Tumbling back into life.

Down the steps of Heaven.
A simple water tap brings you back to Earth.
No water tap, it's the toy of Shiva again!

---

[13] The symbol of the unmanifested form of Shiva (whereas a
statue of Shiva is the manifested form).
[14] Long staff with trident on top (three-pronged spear).

Shiva is back in the water tap
Restraining the water and pushing it with full force
into your face:
Wake up! The play could start to become serious.
Who can stop a freaky foreign girl from running and
dancing and laughing in the streets of Banares?
The Brahmans, the devotees of the holy town, the
shrines in the walls should not be angry.
Is it not simply the Divine ecstasy
Imposed by their all-presiding Lord Shiva?
A woman Sadhu[15] of a Kali temple
Knows to stop the rush of emotions.
Could it be Shiva's consort, Parvati?
The look you share shows a relation from long ago.
"Are you married?" she asked.
"Oh, yes, since today. And the bridegroom is Shiva,
the Lord."
What to answer to such a proud statement.
Consoling eyes follow your crazy dance down the
street.
She might know, how long is the way, how cold, how
odd, how strange,
Slightly remembering her own first ecstasies
Long, long ago.
The lassitude is gone.
Shiva light is ever-present
The embracing of the sunrises becomes more
meaningful;

---

[15] Men and women ascetics who have taken a vow of
renunciation and are dedicated to achieving liberation through
meditation and contemplation of God.

The miracle that happened has to be understood.
Diving deep into the unknown:
Your very, very beautiful nature.
The light you saw, the mantra experienced deep in
your heart,
How could you dare to put it on the lips and make it
heard?
Would it not lose its pristine magnificence and
simplicity?
The treasure is hidden inside, you sit in the corner
And wait and wait and are alert.
Christmas, the holy festival, has come:
Again the old inherited craziness for extravagances
arises.
This day should be your marriage day!
Hundreds of flower garlands for Shiva's beauty.
Down to the end of the ghats[16], toward the middle of
the night
A trembling, ghost-like boy stops your crazy drive
and asks for your hand rings of old relations, to
devote your hands to Shiva.
The Christmas sky is clear.
It opens to millions of golden beams
And fighting happenings of god-like beings.
No empty spot in Heaven;
Where is Shiva to be found?
You quit.
Too much!

---

[16] Stone steps providing access to India's rivers in many cities;
places for bathing, worship, water burial, etc.

Icarus[17] falls back to Earth:
The Lord's first rejection of a crazy ego.
Work hard and simple is the message.
The holy night becomes lonely, cold, and weird.
The familiarity with the Divine has gone,
No more are you invited to the celestial light.
The sorrow is deep, eyes in tears, but unreal,
Walking miles and miles out of the city of liberation.
The morning breeze leads you to Sarnath[18].
An old Brahman shouts, takes the hand of the
neophyte, and orders "Bow down to Lord Buddha!"
The Truth is all,
The special, a dream.
Truth is peace, rest from the lights of celebration in
your mind.
One has to believe and start from the beginning.
All humble, having never touched anybody's feet,
you learn it as an exercise first.
To pull down the images of your fantasy.
It's no use; seek the void as a base to plant the
garden of Paradise.
Simple living with simple tears.
Will the Lord come near again?
Not ready to keep the miracle going,
Wandering in the dust and stone of the ghats,
A Naga Baba[19], all in ash and naked,

---

[17] From Greek Mythology – Icarus, wearing wings of wax, in
ecstasy flies too close to the sun, the wings melt, and he falls
back to Earth.
[18] Buddhist pilgrimage place near Banares (where the newly
Enlightened Buddha gave his first sermon).
[19] Ascetics, followers of Shiva, who are "clothed in space"

Looking over the shoulder, unattached,
Signing to sit and stay:
Shiva himself?
The dreamed-of Guru already?
You can't see. Smiling stupidly against his greatness,
Ignorantly you move away,
His image is marked forever.
You found, but could not recognize.
You leave the City of the Lord
And go away to another Lord: Bodhgaya[20],
Whom you respect and you ask for help.

Buddha? Shiva? Christ?
Buddha and Christ!
Shiva has been your union in moments of Eternity.
The convent for those who lost their husbands
before marriage!
The garland of orange flowers has changed to a self-
chosen maroon Buddhist robe.
Zazen!
Sit in Buddha-mind!
Sit in purity and truth!
The way is not ecstatic, but sincerity and nobleness
wins over.
Still the hope for the future is not gone.
The I Ching oracle on your birthday says:
The great master has to be found.
So true!

___

(naked) and covered in ashes (symbolic of the temporary nature
of the physical body).
[20] Buddhist pilgrimage place where Buddha got Enlightened.

A picture of Kalu Rinpoche of Darjeeling,
The Guru of somebody else,
Reminds you, with his wise beard and the
enlightened eyes, of the vision of your childhood.
Up and away to Darjeeling, but you pause in the St.
Paul's Cathedral in Kolcatta.
You want to worship the Hindu Gods, the Buddha,
But what about your own Christ and the Father?
In the decorated wooden chairs of the empty
cathedral, the Bible has to be read day and night.
Why not repeat the happy days of the Holy
Communion?
A priest in black wants to win you back for the
Christian salvation.
No repentance, sorrow, or guilt.
The light cannot be lost.
In Darjeeling, the ashram doors of a Hindu
Sannyasi[21] yogi opened:
"Stay. Take the initiation of the OM Namah Shivaya
mantra tomorrow."
He is supposed to meditate ten inches above his
asan[22] in the night.

Kalu Rinpoche's disciple invites you for the three
initiations of the Buddhist vehicle.
His Holiness looks deep of love and peace.
A light of white flashes into your heart when given

---

[21] Sannyasi is one who has taken a formal vow (Sannyas) of
renunciation and seeks liberation from reincarnation through
meditation and prayer.
[22] Meditation seat.

the mantra:
OM Mani Padme Hum.
How incredibly proud;
You take the presents of light and sound and a
colored Chenrezee thangkha[23].
What grace has been showered on you, on the way
to the infinite bliss.
Sorry for so much ignorance,
Again you find, but can't appreciate.
You take the mantras and the picture of worship and
go away over the mountains to Kathmandu,
Bodinath, Swayambhu[24]
to share the birthday of the Buddha.
Fifteen days: prostration to the ground a million
times, fasting until boils of impurity grow out of your
body.
Not long ago you played in the Lord's arms of love
and privilege;
Your own craziness throws you out and now you
have to learn hard and wander.

Amarnath[25]
Divine beauty, purity.
Still, temptations draw you back to act in ignorance.
Not yet the readiness to find the teacher to believe
in.
The Guide is there, but you cannot follow

---

[23] Thangkha is a Buddhist painting on silk, here of Chenrezee,
who embodies the compassion of all Buddhas.
[24] Pilgrimage places of Buddhism in Nepal.
[25] Holy pilgrimage place in Kashmir for the worship of Lord Shiva,
Lord of Immortality.

Until the purifications of suffering have eliminated
former karma.
The grace, God Almighty, is always visible
To shower bliss where nobody expects any.
The Divine voice in some fellow friends tells you to
go to Amarnath, the cave of Lord Shiva and Parvati.
You follow the plan and go, invisibly driven towards
the end of the search,
In the company of some people, half observing the
path of renunciation,
Half pulling you down onto the worldly path.
"You can live well and enjoy everything if you keep
your heart religious."
You try the temptation and fall into discomfort,
irritation.
The law of righteousness has to be accepted and
followed, disregarding the worldly path of fake
enjoyment.
Stumbling into bad company on the holy pilgrimage
drives you only closer into the arms of Lord Shiva,
residing in the cave behind the glacier.
The icy winds and waters of immortality
Finally tear you away from worldly relations.

God is near, present, just dive deep into the bliss of
recognition.
You run to the cave where Shiva is waiting for you.
Stupid little girl,
You didn't see that His naked Lordliness was outside,
squatting before the cave
In the form of the two Naga Baba's by the fire:

Shiva and Parvati, the holy principles of Purusha and
Prakriti,
The manifested Shakti and the unmanifested Shiva.
Again you see the same heavenly, extraordinary form
in ash,
Like before, in Banares,
But driven by the conceptions of the mind,
You don't even greet or bow down.
Straight into the cave, towards your well-recognized
place by the side of the small ice lingam of Parvati.
No words of worship, praise, or repentance; who
taught you the language of the Infinite?
Just being, where you always wanted to come back
to.
Time and the restless mind tell you even in Heaven
to go somewhere else.
Although one could always stay in the home of bliss,
Destiny placed the divine manifestation in front of
you. Alas,
The one who cannot recognize has to go down and
search further.
Pilgrimages never go in vain!
God's omnipresence will silently fulfill your unknown
wishes.
You might have even forgotten the message:
"Go and meet the great master."
Innocence of devotion and ecstasy, exhausted in
unknown karma.
You are gifted with the privilege to meet a Guru.
God might not personally save you or bless you, but
all the little cries for help, the desolation, the

suffering due to impurities, and the falsehoods you
are bound to be involved in,
They all attract the mercy of the Lord and liberate
you from the mud and place you into the lotus
flower.
Highest happiness of physical existence was
experienced in the ice blue truths of Amarnath.
The seat of immortality is the never-dying love for
God.

The undisciplined freedom of devotion was going to
be the last expression of the untrained child. Soon
the school of spirituality will begin.
The tears of ecstasy will change to unbelievable pain,
And again be transformed into the joys of
purification.

All the way up to Amarnath body and mind are
constantly crying for the union with Shiva,
misunderstanding or mixing up the Absolute in
different planes.
The attendants of Shiva are all around, invisible, yet
everywhere in the pilgrim place area.
One of them could have taken too much
inappropriate interest in a young girl's ecstasy, which
might cause him to fall down to Earth and see the
limitations and consequences of the mortal plane.
Only one lifetime required, to give liberation by
becoming the Guru of a seeking girl's soul.
The price is high.
Complications cannot be avoided on the mortal

plane.
The Divine Drama is rolling: things happen, some
stories are played out.
And everything looks normal and understandable.
From Amarnath the body went down,
The head still sparkling from Divine intoxication:
So much grace of light and devotion.
Again worldly influences overpower through lack of
discrimination.
Only the Guru will make clear the different paths of
the real and the unreal.
The way is pointed out straight to Haridwar.
Even when you don't know anything, the Divine is
teaching you constantly
To recognize and remember later on.
Fear of losing His Grace will keep you determined on
the right path.
Somehow an orange robe is put on you, the heavy
volume of Sri Aurobindo's <u>On Yoga</u> was carried
around without ever reading it.
The blanket was taken away,
A little sleeping bag survived.
One amulet with a happy picture of your family could
not be just thrown away.
"Go to Haridwar or Rishikesh, the land of the Gurus."
The only positive advice from the more or less
spoiling company of travelers.

THREE

Arrival

This time you leave all friends, adventure, and
desperate searches.
Longing for protection from distractions and
impurities,
Empty-hearted, you arrive at Haridwar-Maya Puri,
the City of Illusion.
To overcome the unreal, enter the Truth at
Hari-ka-dwar, the Gate of Heaven.
"You can stay in Prem Nagar (City of Love), an
ashram where all foreigners stay, south of Haridwar."
You ask the way,
But the voice of destiny points out the opposite way,
north of Haridwar.
The vibrations of the holy city work hard on you.
An unknown depression and heaviness comes over
you,
A strong urge of freeing yourself from a long-carried
burden.
To whom to give it, who will take it?
The Ganga calls you nearer, awaiting you.
The ghats are crowded, but with spiritual pressure.
The nectar of the holy place cannot be tasted yet by
the newcomer.
Saints and so-called Saints all over.
The spiritual image could not be more different from

the normal world.
Beggars pulling at your bag, "bakshish, bakshish.[26]"
The arrival in the dreamland of your childhood!
Oh, to give away all, to give up everything all
together, only to live somewhere in peace.
The way through Haridwar seems to be more
purgatory than the Gate of Heaven.
Some suspect youths follow you with bad remarks.
A bridge to an island promises trees, the Ganga all
around,
A place to weep and weep yourself away with all
your past.
Will it be so easy to dissolve yourself into the Ganga?
You gave yourself a limit of up to twenty-four years
to find some sense in life.
If you cannot, it will be more reasonable to finish this
play of ups and downs forever.
Is Heaven where you die to this world?
Walking heavily further,
Eyes swollen,
Driven into the unknown Paradise.

You don't know, but finally you arrive.
The Great Master
Is already awaiting you.
Sitting for years on the island by the fire, meditating,
for the will of Ma Ganga to appear.
One year ago, in the fall, when you received the call
to start for India,

---

[26] A cry asking for alms: "Donations! Presents!"

The Divine play had given the fakir[27] by the Ganga, a
vision of the Holy Mother in her celestial form:
No clothes, but covered all over with brilliant jewelry.
"Son, tell me what you want?"
"Nothing Ma of the wealth you are offering.
"Let me stay, for lives and lives at Your gate, but
always having enough to serve the people who come
to me.
"Stay with me in a form that nobody can take away."
"Tathasthu." (So let it be.)
The Guru, in conscious sleep, awakens to accept the
divine play.
Compassion starts its power.
"There she comes, the promise of the Ganga:"
The Divine has become mortal,
More or less miserable, and
Full of complications, as the future will show.
It is difficult to recognize the Divine on Earth,
because It is bound to accept the dressing of this
creation.
On a September afternoon,
The Guru recognizes His disciple
Arriving over the bridge onto His island of twenty
years of asceticism,
Closely followed by evil forces.
A desolated form of Maya,
Obviously ready to surrender to the next best
solution.

---

[27] A Sufi term: an Enlightened One, One who loves God and
Sacrifices all for God. Like Hindu Sadhu, renounces family,
wealth, physical comforts, everything to unite with God.

"There she is coming." He says to His English-
speaking devotee. "Tell her to sit here."
And there you arrive, blind to the situation around.
Like one who is hypnotized, you follow the call to
come and sit down.
Called a hundred times, but never able to follow!
How simple:
Just believe the order and sit and find and survive.
The evil forces vanish at once.
This is the place you will never leave.
The small island will represent the whole world.

Your Guru
An almost naked human being, a Saint,
Unknown, strange, and black to you,
Will mold your emotions to a complete surrendering.
Truth will become established in one moment
without knowing it,
Chosen by the Guru when the time is right according
to the constellation of cause and reaction.
The divinity looked at you, touched you with His
soul;
Unaware of what is happening,
You have come to be new born.
Not reborn by the will of samsara[28],
But admission has been granted by your heavenly
parents into the
Guru School of purification,
Which, if you pass,

---

[28] The soul's cycle of birth, mutability, death and rebirth.

Leads to the final examination:
Freedom by the knowledge of the Self.
The Guru will be the being in front of you:
A celestial being in the form of an Indian Naga Baba:
the naked one, the Avadhut[29], the ever-free, living in
the world without being bound to its attachments.
A Fakir, without parentage, without possession,
without being literate,
The tamasic[30], cruel form of Shiva and his
attendants, wild, angry, unsentimental, sacrificing,
fighting for the truth, dying for the justification of the
Atman[31].
You don't have to look at His appearance, you
perceive the divine being and respond with an
unknown comfort in the heart.
A smile is growing from inside
A knowing without words:
Company with Truth.
The September breeze, life-giving trees, the all-
promising flow of the powerful, rain-filled Ganga; the
Earth, purified by cow dung to beautify the
surroundings of the duni fire[32] with it's incarnation:
one majestic flame satisfied by the service of
valuable teak wood.

---

[29] An enlightened being who has risen above body-
consciousness, duality, and worldly concerns.
[30] Tamas is one of the three gunas (qualities of nature): the
quality of darkness, ignorance, and inertia. Tamasic is descriptive
of tamas.
[31] Soul, the true innermost Self of everything.
[32] Sacred fire of the Sadhu, like a temple; the fire is never
allowed to burn out.

All the elements, beauty and harmony, fulfilled by
the crown of all manifestations, the human being,
the Saint, glowing in a deep brown golden body after
a bath in the immortal nectar of the Ganga.
One loincloth wrapped around loosely, the grace of
the limbs, thin like the branches of the tree, a
movement of pranic[33] flow, not a body with different
parts:
Oneness of controlled energy.
No words to describe this body of Truth, the
Brahman, manifested lightness, and love,
A heavenly plantation,
The end of poetry.
The long waving beard, the ever-old by having no
age,
The beard of the seer, from the dreams of your
heavenly heritage!
Your eyes close to experience this final happiness:
You have met with the truth of existence.
Not a physical image, as in Banares.
You will be allowed to live this truth.
The white cows around close the circle of this
heavenly garden.
Just born, ignorant,
But you will know, step by step.
Slowly by yourself you recover from a broken being
to a blessed innocent smiling one.
What happened?
Who freed you from the unbearable burden?

---

[33] Prana is the life force, so refers to movement of pure life force.

Has the suicide happened already and you passed into Heaven?
Life is born anew without a past.
There is a king to whom all this Island's beauty and simplicity belong to, to whose brilliance everyone is attending, and your own little existence will join the service of sacrifice.

The light of the day goes down. Rain starts.
One dares to move out of the experience of bliss.
Save yourself into meditation, to inquire what happened.
What could make this unknown being more familiar than your own heart?
Heavy rain brings you back to the fire,
To sit near this glowing beauty of the supernatural.
You need no escape any more.
You have got a place, a home for your soul to grow up to spiritual maturity.
No words of conventional conversation.
Nobody asks your name, home, and what you are doing.
But He, His Holiness without attributes, looks at you from the inner Self,
Knows all of you, by knowing the supreme truth and illusion,
Ready to play the game on Earth following the heavenly orders.
The bliss will stay,
The form has changed.
The Ascetic is blessed with the toy of a female child!

Not aware of coming consequences, the arrival is celebrated with extra thanks for Mother Ganga.
Your first Aarti Puja[34], an evening meal in the light of the moon, and the running presence of Ganga waves.

Coming Home
Never had such a stillness been experienced.
You cannot talk when you finally come home after such senseless wandering.
"Go and spread your sleeping bag by the side of the Ganga ghats."
Final bliss as a worldly heavenly dream.
Free and protected,
Love without touch,
The beauty of reality,
Ganga Mata's[35] waves sing you to sleep.
Tomorrow will be your first birthday;
Life itself has become the most precious present.
The promise of the light of Shiva, the oneness of the many, can be experienced.
Before dawn a whole eternity of events.
You are drawn down to the platform by the Ganga.
Rain in the middle of the night.
The residing God calls to the night meditation by the fire.
Yes and there you find them, the fairy tale saints who sit in lotus position to join their soul with the

---

[34] Aarti is fire worship. Puja is worship of the Divine through invocations, prayers, songs, and rituals.
[35] The Mother, Her Divine form in the Ganga river.

Supreme.

The high priests offer to Shiva the Supreme all happiness, beauty, and knowledge.

The humans try to worship and meditate on the mantra, and in the purity of the heart you are the lowest one, knowing the name, but unable to pronounce it.

You encourage yourself into the position, but lose the balance like an infant who tries to sit or stand.

You tumble down, overcome by tamas in heaviness and drowsiness.

The burning will is there, but the flesh has a long way to go.

The rain stops and everybody moves to his place by the Ganga.

The Baba, the Saint, holds the position glowing in oneness with the fire and the darkness of the night.

The rest vanishes into unconsciousness.

After no time at all,

Again you are awakened. What now? It is still night!

The god is giving His morning example:

Cleaning the fire, sweeping the platform, feeding the cows, the auspicious bath. He shouts His morning worship straight to Heaven, vibrating all over the area "Gange Hare, Narmade Hare, Jata Shankare, Hare Hare Mahadev[36]!"

Only the sounds of the water in the morning purity, God and His servant devotee have become one.

---

[36] Mantras for bath in the holy Ganga.

The mystery is not over.

The vibration leaves you in the dreaming state,
unable to move.
Witness to the unimaginable.
Again the powerful call of the conch pushes you into
the heavenly reality:
Datt, Datt, Datt, Datta, Datta[37], three times, waking
everything up, down to the most hidden cells of your
being:
That is the conch that can give enlightenment and
death equally!
You have no courage to move or wake up for any
activity like bathing or meditation.
Here the divine is so near, in complete harmony with
the fire, the Ganga, the cows, and the rising morning
star.
Alone, resting in the Self,
Who dares to breathe,
Not to disturb the glimpse of eternity.
You realize the heavenly book has opened.
You will become a part of the fairy tale.
The waves of the Ganga cannot be separated from
the river goddess.
You share in the activities of the day, you explore the
island.
It is sealed: you have found your Guru, the only love
of your life.
Change, new birth, has taken place.

---

[37] Mantras for blowing the conch.

And then He calls out your name: "Narvada[38]."
Sitting on the steps of the Ganga you are smashed
by this power-blessing.
This can only be your own specific name!
The morning invocation of an ascetic is accepted in
its manifested form:
"He Narvade."
It is a call that will enter your heart at any time, at
any place.
Consciously you are born into your destination.
You got a name, a heavenly parentage:
The Guru as the mother of compassion, forgiveness,
care;
The father to force the discipline;
The friend to play with and enjoy,
Transferring all necessary knowledge,
Making you His disciple, you will become an official
heir of the supreme treasure.

"Have you made the Baba your Guru?
"In one day?"
"Yes!"
"We have lived all our lives in Haridwar and have not
yet found a Guru" an English-speaking devotee asks
you, full of curiosity and excitement.
Yes, the acknowledgement took place naturally, in no
time.

An unknown happiness of security and freedom

---

[38] Given name, corresponding to the sacred river Narmada.

starts spreading all over your being.
How could this happen?
Not knowing any name or heritage,
Only Shiva, the one without a name and a thousand names,
The one without a family, the not-born, the one without possessions or ambitions.
Birth took place where questions and doubts are no longer valuable:
A change from confusion, ignorance, suffering, and unhappiness
To clarity, right understanding, and happiness, even in suffering.
OM Guruji!
Your inborn nature, you are always meeting in different forms.
No words are necessary to make you known to one another.
All that happens will be to remember your past, back to your celestial origin.
No fear of the unknown: what will happen is the truth of both aspects: positive and negative.
One starts to recognize that everything is the grace of Ganga, God, the Guru:
His will in all and everything.
Thereby starts the final stage into becoming a God-child forever through growing, unshakable faith.
Faith is God.
"Shiv, Shiv" is the truth – all else is false!
These two mantras will be the heart of the teaching for the next years, if not for the whole life:

Faith is God; Shiva, His name is Truth; and all else is
false.
Yes, this is the Guru, the manifested form on Earth
from the vision in Banares!
When the Guru transfers the Shiva mantra into your
being, His glowing dark being opens to a deepness of
unrealizable beauty.
You close your eyes and sink into this ocean of bliss
where knowledge is no longer important.
Our union took place through the recognition of the
individual soul of the Supreme Soul.
Shiva is the union,
The separation is the past.
Now life has changed.
Long, endless, sittings by the Ganga.
No work left.
The highest action – the work on the Soul.

Day and night, whenever or wherever, under the
tree, alone in the forest,
Your inner being is always there where you belong:
Shiva, Shiva, Shiva.
And Shiva is the Guru, your mother and father in the
spiritual childhood,
The book of knowledge when you become ready to
learn,
The dissolution of the form into the Supreme, when
your renouncement has ripened.
OM Sri Guruve Namah![39]

---

[39] Prostration mantra to the Guru.

No words, no humans, can gratify the splendor and greatness of the Guru.

The form has become divine by the faith that took birth.
Faith has power that no science can prove.
A stone turns into a human form, acting as punishment or blessing.
The truthful, simple Sadhu in cow service by the Ganga, illiterate, angry, in ash and no clothes, has opened up understanding into the mystical nature of Shiva: the tamasic, destructive force, absorbing poison,
The snake of desire around the neck,
Living in the cremation ground, hiding the splendor of the soul behind the body of flesh and blood.
Unknown, not respected, inconvenient to most –
But a God of Truth to the dreaming girl in search of all the treasures and pleasures of this world.
His poverty makes Him the king of the clouds and the waves of the Ganga, with the wind as His gown.
Guruji Digambar[40]!
His illiteracy shows the silent prophet whose wisdom is beyond all knowledge of the books.
His anger will be welcomed as the destroyer of all obstacles, for the goal of purification.
There is no end to His virtues, which often appear to be vices to the world,
Opposite to general values.

---

[40] Digambar is one who is clad in space, the four directions.

What is pleasant for the world has to be renounced
in the spiritual realm: what comes first on Earth will
be the last in Heaven.
His appearance becomes a treasure house of purity,
omnipotence, and wisdom:
A vision, a manifested divinity for you.
Only for you –
A Guru, the blessing of God, only for you.

The first privilege when you enter the heavenly home
is that absolutely everything is infused with the
fragrance of Truth,
The unchangeable, rightness.
If your Guru is like this, it is wonderful, a miracle, a
blessing.
If it would have been the opposite, how great and
auspicious too.
Complete acceptance: a state that never had been
achieved before in your drama-filled life of illusion,
confusion, and insecurity.
A life of dangers and risks indeed.
The jungle has been passed with all its wild and
terrifying animals of desires and temptations.
The seasonal dream state has cleared up.
The Ganga of wisdom is flowing, purifying the
obstacles.
Now you have entered Hari-ka-dwar, the Gate of
Heaven;
Left behind is Maya Puri, the City of Illusion.
How lucky: you have escaped! What a pleasure, to
sleep in front of the heavenly gate.

A lifetime for the look into paradise of renunciation or
to be the chosen next to be called inside to meet the
Lord.
The Lord of Lords: Shiva.
Ram is Shiva, Shiva is Krishna, and Krishna is Ram.
Gauri Shankar, Radhe Sham!

FOUR

Divine Ecstasy

The Beginning
Divine ecstasy.
Certainly to be achieved, but it doesn't last or it
changes its form into the ordinary, lacking ecstasy.
Work, washing the place, sweeping, feeding,
cleaning the cows, etc.
The broom becomes your teacher to teach you
purification.
The platform becomes your body and mind to be
cleaned, therefore you sweep and sweep and forget
the whys and how much.
What a pleasure to clean the glass from which your
Guru has drunk.
You would suffer were someone else to have done it.
The brass glasses and pots become golden in the
morning sun.
You are not washing; Ganga Mata is polishing and
you watch and learn and play and listen.
Eternities are spent washing the dishes.
Meanwhile the Ganga shows you around in Her
heavenly kingdom.
Babaji, Guruji is watching His child growing as she
brings buckets of water or a single glass.
Soon she will start to speak the mantras
remembering her Indian heritage. Shiva Shiva Shiv.

Inside and outside, awake and asleep.
Shiva, Shiva everywhere: present in the Ganga, in
the jungle, in the sky, in the cows, in the people.
Freedom unknown,
Boundless joy of the child,
For some, unlimited time.
Happy to live in Shiva, and to receive and give back.
Serving holy cows, roaming around with them on the
island until evening, has become the fulfillment of
your childhood dream.
Alone with the cows under the sky by the water,
alone with the trees and the earth.
Sleeping beneath the stars, being woken up by the
brightness of the moon.
Eating what is found in the Earth or dropped by the
birds,
Talking with the winds and weeping with the rains.
Soon this paradise of spiritual, sensual pleasures will
have to change from the form to the formless.
Your enthusiasm will calm down.
Your youth becomes weak in search of the Truth
beyond happiness and suffering.

The surrender to Guruji takes place the day after the
historical meeting.
The divine will arranged for you, for Baba, for the
fire, the cows, the Ganga, the mantra.
It will last as long as the divine play lasts.
It is part of the grace; nothing in this world will be
able to separate you from the divine.
The unshakable faith and your love seem to touch

the summits of Sita to Ram and Ram to Sita.
The joy, the thanksgiving, the power of endurance.
Everything that might happen, even the worst, will
be turned to nectar by this love and faith.
What a miracle that this obstinate world, so full of
confusion, enemies, quarrels, and jealousies could
change so imperceptibly, into a life of sense and
truth, harmony and understanding.
Not only the present shines under the veil of
righteousness, but also the terrible path.
Wonderful, the controversies are finished; what
remains is a smile, a sleep, a dream in bliss.

How to overcome sleep at three in the morning. The
bath at the feet of Mother Ganga, the colder the
water, the warmer her blessings,
And the crest jewel of your new birth land:
The meditation!
Sitting behind the master, His snake-like silhouette
against fire and Ganga water.
"Shiva, Shiva," all love and joyful discipline,
concentration on top of the head.
That is all for a lifetime to understand.
Guruji's mission was highest in this simplicity.
All the Vedas in one syllable, "OM, Shiv, Shiva OM"
Repeat with all the enthusiasm of your life energy!
A treasured infinity of the mantra.
Shiva, and nothing else.
Libraries have been written on God, OM, Shiv,
Without coming to the end of the explanation.
All the knowledge of the learned and experienced

has to bow down to submit to Guruji's simple and
final "Shiv."

A prophet without lectures and fame,
Years of teaching, listening to the silent
inexhaustible, unexplainable "Shiv Shiv Shiv."
The Guru: the divine manifestation of God.
This is the method to show you the way to the
Supreme,
Omniscient and without form.
From Guru as father and mother, to your individual
Guru, then renouncing them all for the imperishable
oneness of truth and wisdom.
"Only through me can you come to the Father."
Jesus said.
A Guru for you alone, not famous and respected by
the world, but for you He became Shiva, a renunciate
on Earth, untouchable, yet at the same time so near
as to be a reflection of His very being.
"How can you make a poor Fakir your Guru?" the
women from town ask,
"So wild and angry, not knowing the scriptures, no
place to stay, wearing the loin cloth from the
crematory fires, standing in line with the beggars."
"Yes, yes" you laugh...knowing more about His
heavenly beauty.
The world will be against us, the Guru and the
disciple,
Attacks and insults, but the Guru will remain the
divine as long as the disciple's faith is unshakable.
Once you have recognized the Supreme in the form,

how can you fall into ignorance again?
The form may change to a higher experience, but
the wisdom will remain the same.
Jai Guru dev! Hail to the Guru!

The first months in your kingdom are heaven without
restriction.
You leave everything behind, all plays of the past,
sin, bad karma, books, knowledge, and qualifications.
How beautiful that nobody ever asked your name,
family, education.
A last formal responsibility, a letter to your mother,
contains the cruel words that you have found a
heaven that doesn't need anything anymore, for now
and forever.
No power can bring you away from here.
The letter is sent and you feel the right to fall into
Ganga Mata's arms and pray to be locked up in Her
paradise.

Guru, Cows, and Ganga
It is the love of the Guru that presented you the
beautiful embrace of the Ganga and the motherly
advice from the cow mothers.
The cows cover an important part in your spiritual
schooling.
One reason certainly they are called holy.
The Guru, the cows, and the Ganga
Become the teaching through their silent presence.
Truth is all around. You meditate and you find the
divine smile is protecting you.

"Go with the cows and nothing evil will happen to
you."
Sitting all day, alone in the jungle, under a tree,
Soon falling into meditation surrounded by the quiet
regurgitation of the cows.
The gentle oldest one of them, called the
grandmother cow or Dadi,
Would rest her huge head on your shoulder, from
behind, continuing to move the mouth as she chews,
Seeming to give advice from her large eyes,
Murmuring with streams of tears:
"You are not alone, my child, we are all weeping
here on Earth, but cheer up, the Ganga and the Baba
are with you."
All the mothers of your terrestrial lives unite together
in the cow Mata:
Warmth and love that consoles your heart.
The Dadi cow is always there to give advice and
encouragement.
Quickly you learn that hiding behind the cow always
works wonders, and in the nights, in the depths of
your loneliness, God, the body, and the sentiments
seek shelter by curling up under the neck of the
never-ever sleeping cow Mata.

Slowly, slowly, your body starts revolting against its
negligence and defeat by the exalted mind.
Living on whatever the Ganga gives is great, but still
the sacrifice is going to the bones.
One chai in the morning before going with the cows;
One in the afternoon after coming back with the

cows.
Perhaps somebody brings something in the daytime,
but mostly not.
Still one meal at night for everybody.
And for us,
The maker Babaji, one disciple more, and yourself,
whatever is left over.
You happily take all the pots and plates to the Ganga
and have a celestial meal with the stars and the Gods
of heaven.
The sacrifice of staying hungry all day turns the
whole meal into gold and silver and nectar.
All the musicians of your senses rejoice in
supernatural tunes,
And indescribable satisfaction makes you enjoy the
kingly meal of actually nothing important: dal, roti,
and chawal[41].

Make yourself poor and empty and riches will flood
over you.
And Babaji, Guruji, His Santosh, contentment, has
always been blameless.
The Ganga gives everyday, everyday for all – the
cows, the people, the birds, the insects.
It is as if Guruji would produce everything out of the
waves of the Ganga:
Chai and meals, sometimes apples and sweets, other
times special people, friends and foes, musicians, or
other entertainers appear out of Ganga's Maya.

---

[41] Dal - dried beans cooked with spices, roti - round flat wheat
bread, and chawal – rice, are three staples of the Indian diet.

All God's illusionary play!
Living by the Ganga,
Naturally everything appears as Ganga's
manifestation:
What you get and what not, what you eat and what
not,
The happiness and joy you receive or the
complications, sufferings, and worldly attacks.
But what can go wrong if all you see is divine play?

Once, in the jungle, you feel frightened by someone
with an axe, trying to stop and harass you. Behold!
His eyes are the ones of your Guruji! You can only
fold your hands and pay respect and turn away and
go in happiness without fear.
The snakes that appear become Shiva's attendants,
you bow down to their beauty in frightening grace,
Snakes of heavenly greens and yellows, basking in
the light that gives them their color.
It is as if Guruji had opened His hidden collection just
for you and nobody else.

One time coming back with the cows, the dark clouds
are already announcing some unpleasant game: a
group of people lead by the so-called "opposition
Sadhu," (the one who always tried to attack you with
pain in order to destroy the truth of your being).
Your Babaji, graceful and indifferent in the middle of
them, like one going to an execution.
You are alone in front as terrifying members of the
world capture the heavenly being whose child you

are.

The drama goes on: shouting, danger, quarrel,
Guruji squats down and is beaten with sticks.
"They are beating your Guru, you don't do
anything?"
For a second you think "Shall I interfere?" Oh no,
Guruji's eyes are Santosh – self-contented as ever.
The powerful Ganga waves are smiling and
encouraging.
"Who can beat your Guru?
Shiva, the Atman, immortal forever!"
What fools we are all, what a circus.
The world is all-powerful but the mantra OM Namah
Shivaya, Shiva, Shiva is your heartbeat.
Nothing else to do than to sink down by the next tree
and close your eyes and meditate.
All this divine play, voices of the enemies, shouts of
anger, nothing more than sensations in a fake game
and again silence.
The silence, the beauty of faith has survived.
Sometimes God makes you react in a successful way,
and sometimes you are bound to fail the examination
when you involve yourself in Maya.

FIVE

Stories

The Cobra
You remember a story Guruji always kept telling from His fakir time.
Once roaming deeper into the jungle on the other side of the Ganga, surrounded by the smell of strong hemp plants, all of a sudden a huge cobra stood up in front of Him, looking straight into the eyes. Even the heart of a Saint might stop beating in front of death. Hands are folded together. "Maharaj, I did not know that you are living here, otherwise I would never have come here, forgive me."
Silence, no word, no breath, awaiting the bite of destiny.
After some time He opened His eyes, just to see the black long tail disappearing into the forest.
Hari Om tat sat.

The Fawn
The jungle has always been a place for beings living outside human society:
Either the Sadhu seeking to live in solitude in search of truth, or the criminal, to hide from the law.
One time, also on the other side of the Ganga, where the jungle is full of wild animals like cobras, elephants, deer, pumas, boars, and tigers, Babaji

happened to catch a little fawn. At once from nowhere, three or four "suspect" people surrounded Him and asked Him to give the deer to them, already enjoying the coming meal.

Babaji, all alone, held the frightened animal tight in His arms, not giving up His position, whatever might happen.

What to do, the situation was dangerous. "I won't give the deer to you, but if you can catch it when I set it free, then what can I do?"

The group was ready, standing all in a circle, thinking it is an easy task to catch the little scared deer.

Babaji, with urgency in the heart to save the animal, clapped His hind side strongly, "Go, run for your life!" God is always with the good intention.

In one second the deer leapt high over the heads of its killers, and the next minute it was far away.

Ganga Mata ki jai!

The Deer

Another time in the jungle, Babaji surprised a person who was binding a freshly caught deer.

Looking up, seeing the naked form of a Saint, he dropped his hands off the animal, which at once ran away. He stood then with folded hands, asking forgiveness.

Humbleness excuses even heavy sins.

The man, who was posted in Haridwar, wanted to make a little extra money.

"How blessed you are, being posted at a holy place like Haridwar, and even being paid for it, where rich

people have to pay dearly to stay only for a day."
Babaji's words and presence opened his eyes, his life
was changed – he became a devotee for the rest of
his life.

The Sadhu
Roaming around in search of some food, Babaji met
with a Sadhu in deep meditation sitting by the
Ganga.
Time went on and Babaji offered to bring some food
from the next village, miles away.
"Oh no, just wait a minute, I will bring something."
Saying so, the Sadhu disappeared into the jungle.
Babaji ready to wait for a long time, laid down to
rest. The other Saint soon reappeared with a basket
of fresh cooked food, more than the mind could
imagine.
The smile of supreme power in the face of the one,
the smile of complete faith on the other.
The more one surrenders to the divine, the more the
supernatural is visible in the natural.
Sadhus have laid down everything at the lotus feet of
the lord.

Fasting
Whatever happens is the divine will and therefore is
happily and confidently accepted.
Guruji had come to the banks of the Ganga to give
up this worldly life, to put all his life energy into His
divine hands: if God wanted him to live, he would
live, if not, he was prepared to accept the death of
the body.

Babaji always praised the grace of the Ganga at least
once a day; she gives food and other necessities to
all beings equally.
A day without any food Guruji happily accepted as a
higher blessing than to eat.
Sadhus live from what God gives them, the fast
naturally occurs when God refuses to give.
Not choosing austerities, but suffering hardships
when God wants them to suffer.

Often Guruji remembered one of the few "fasting
days" in Ganga Mata's kingdom.
The day was gray and cold, without any devotees
who felt like donating anything to a poor Sadhu.
The only small donation of the day had been used for
the cows' grass, as it was His life habit never to eat,
or to serve others, before the cows had eaten.
This was one vow, the other was never to eat until at
least five or ten people from outside had been
served.
Babaji, as usual full Santosh[42], thanked Ganga Mata
for the wonderful day and laid down to fall into His
sleepless sleep.
In the middle of the night, the sweet voice of an
elderly woman in a whitish sari woke Him up.
"My son, wake up and eat your bread."
True or a dream – so often we live where the real
and the unreal meet.
Babaji got up and was fed by Ganga Mother's loving

---

[42] Contentment

hand.

What supernatural happiness for a rough Sadhu,
fighting His whole life against comfort and emotion:
Ma had brought a basket of fresh homemade foods
of all possible varieties.

You are never alone; Ma is always there to comfort
your longing for love.

Give up even the last trace of desires and the divine
in the form of the unexpected will surprise you.

The Lord is enjoying His sports in this world.

The Ruin

Another time in the middle of the night Babaji yells:
"Ma where are you putting me?" In a dream, Ma
had taken Him in her arms and placed Him in a weird
ruin, somewhere in the Ganga jungle, full of snakes
and scorpions.

Guruji forgot about the dream, but one year later,
the will of Mother Ganga made Him search for an
ashram place and, lo! He was led to that very ruin:
an abandoned dharmsala[43] which was meant to
become the later "Santosh Puri Ashram."

The Power of Faith

On the island or from the jungle, often strange or
asocial people passed our fireplace.

One night a drunkard arrived, took out a big shiny
knife, and sat by the fire.

"Baba, get yourself ready, I am just doing my job."

---

[43] Simple free, or very cheap, housing, usually offered by a
temple or ashram.

Guruji, all alone with the situation, decided to sit by the Ganga: if somebody could change the situation, then Ganga Mata could.

Calling urgently, reciting the Mantra, and calling Shiva's name into the night, He managed to bring the devil to tears like a child.

The arrogance, pride, and violence melted away into devotion and repentance.

A little helping push and the veil of ignorance lifted, Simplicity and truth is revealed.

The person had come, drunk with tamas and violence, to kill a Saint;

In the presence of Guru and Ganga Mata, he had been freed from his darkness and became a lifelong devotee.

Satyug, the age of truth, in the middle of the Kaliyug, the age of darkness.

One remembers the stories of the ancient Rishis[44] taming wild animals to live peacefully together in the ashram.

The power of truth and faith, turning thoughts into flowers, poison into nectar.

Ganga Mata's Maya, or Guruji's Maya, always liked to be full of surprises, such as a frightening event, revealing the divine sun underneath.

Once your illusion is destroyed, the play of divine consciousness becomes obvious everywhere.

---

[44] The wise Enlightened forefathers of Vedic (Indian spiritual) Tradition.

Cow Seva[45]

Sadhus are Mahatmas – great souls whose compassion and love is so realized that other beings' pain becomes their own suffering.

One of Guruji's determinations, like an order of God, was to serve the cows, if necessary by sacrificing His own life.

In Haridwar, some winters are soft and pleasant and others are ice cold, stormy, and rainy.

All the privileged inhabitants of Haridwar, and all the Sadhus, have a rough and dry time of hardships in winter, which will be rewarded in spring and summer when devotees are visiting the town to shower donations on Sadhus, beggars, and the poor.

In the winter, Guruji sometimes would point out places in the jungle to dig out some sweet roots to eat, or big logs of wood from a flood years ago to keep the fire going.

The God of Fire, a visible, physical manifestation of the divine like the sun, the moon, and the elements, must be worshipped every morning and evening, and decorated with flowers and leaves, its place pasted with cow dung.

Babaji created the most beautiful living temple out of the arrangements of wood from the Ganga and the jungle, sometimes even sandalwood.

The ornamental design in the white ash and the flames would light up the whole area.

---

[45] Service.

Seva to the fire, Guruji said, and the cow service are all wish-fulfilling and provide the necessities of the day.

Once when there was nothing, not even for the cows, Babaji, suffering for them, filled with growing anger. He loudly and obstinately took the axe and cut branches from a tree.
The hollow sound of the axe called all over the area in the winter dryness.
"First the fire has to get its food, then the rest will follow!"
And so it was: as soon as the fire was burning brightly, some officers from the island nearby arrived in a hurry. "Baba, what happened? No wood to burn? Shanti Shanti[46], we will send some, and wheat and grass also."
Guruji's anger calmed, because the service of the cows and the fire were secured.

In search of food, one disciple of Guruji promised to be back in an hour with food and the like. How?
His austerity was to go to the bathing ghats and for an hour to dive in the ice-cold Ganga water. He would come up with some coins, or sometimes even some gold and silver that the devotees had offered to the Holy Mother. Enough for the next meal and the grass for the cows.

---

[46] Peace.

Guruji's way of teaching is beyond logic:
He got extremely angry in order to express His
suffering that the cows were supposed to stay
hungry, and promised to leave the place if the Ganga
did not bring food for the cows and the people
immediately.
With unshakable determination He lay down under
His cloth by the Ganga.
Something had to happen, so all the devotees,
especially you, meditated and prayed with the
highest intensity: OM Namah Shivaya.
And lo! God always listened to your prayer: some
devotee arrived from somewhere to calm down
Guruji's divine anger. Or, one time the postman had
to arrive with an unexpected money order, Jai Ganga
Ma.

Sometimes the knot of difficulties just opened by a
miracle of a divine sign, but sometimes, because of
decreasing devotion, you had to go to some people
and ask for money for the cows; if they refused, you
had to go to the next one. There must be food for
the cows.
Or you had to go through Haridwar to a dairy to ask
for two sacks of grass on credit.
If someone refused the exchange of ten rupees for
the grass, besides not being able to give, the next
day it was possible that he got a tax bill for ten
thousand rupees.
If you do not give voluntarily, then you will have to
give by force!

No Tents!

For the cows, Guruji arranged some tent canvas as protection against the cold wind and rain. We had the fire to sit and warm ourselves or one sack-like blanket which could be folded four times to become thicker. The newborn cows stayed with us by the fire. The mother cow, named Ganga, who was sick with fever, stayed in the tents behind us.

Before a coming Kumbha Mela[47], it is the rule to clean all Haridwar of huts and tents. One cold rainy winter morning, the police in charge came and the officer forced Babaji to pull down the tents and go to some dharmsala.

"I can go but where will the cows go?" The officer became hard and harder and insisted on taking the tents away. Guruji's sorrow for the freezing cows, especially the sick Ganga cow, knew no limits.

One saw His heart breaking; He had no defense other than to burst out in anger against the hard-hearted officer. "If my cow dies, your son will die!"

"Go, Baba go, I have heard many poor fakirs, talking like this."

What's said is said.

The officer went away with the tent and Babaji in His one loincloth, the wooden sandals, and a thin shawl, in a fury went to Delhi to get another tent as

---

[47] Kumbha Mela is a sacred Hindu pilgrimage that takes place at the following four locations of India every twelve years: Allahabad-Prayag, Haridwar, Ujjain, and Nasik. It is the largest gathering of humanity in the world: Saints, Sadhus, pilgrims.

protection for the cows. Delhi is twice as cold as
other places. He got the tent from some devotee,
but almost died from the cold. Baba arrived at the
bus stand so cold, He was unable to move His hands.
By the will of the Ganga, a devotee recognized Babaji
and picked Him up in his arms and brought Him into
the station, shouting: "My Guruji has come, my
Lord, my owner has come!" In no time he gathered
all the papers from the bookstores and warmed
Babaji with fire and tea.
When Guruji came back to Haridwar to the island, He
just called the cow. "Ganga I am coming."
The cow looked up, lifted the head and body, to fall
down and die. We all collapsed as well. The
struggle went on for the cows and for ourselves.
The next day, the son of the officer was riding his
cycle along the Ganga. He fell down and the handle
of the bicycle hit him on his head. He died on the
spot.
The officer's whole family came to apologize, brought
back the tents and promised that Babaji could even
build a hut on the island, with their permission.
Babaji kept quiet, somehow also sorry, but what to
do, the Ganga had fulfilled His curse.
It is said, the one who surrenders only for one year
to Mother Ganga, whatever he speaks becomes true.

The Flood and the Wood
In India you are always close to nature and
depending on nature's laws and its extravagances in
the form of flood, droughts, earth quakes, dam

breaks, and the like. One year made history because of the flood caused by the Alaknanda River dam break.

Disaster all over, the water was yellow with mud, overflowing the island with wood, huts, utensils, and dead bodies of animals, people, and fish.

During the flood, Guruji, in spite of all attempts to get Him evacuated, survived on the island, spending the time in a tree, even taking the fire with Him. The cows had been brought to a safer place. No hardship is forever, so somehow He survived, nature calmed down and the situation normalized.

The Sadhus enjoyed the immense gain of wood, big piles for the coming winter. Soon the town people came with horses and donkeys to carry the wood away to sell.

Guruji watched over two big piles of wood for the Sadhus to do austerities in the fire fragrance.

One day a stout wood dealer arrived. He tried to involve Guruji in some sweet conversation. Guruji, Himself all truth throughout, quickly sensed some falsehood. Looking behind to the other side of the island where Sadhus had their fireplace, He saw that horses and donkeys were about to carry away the wood which had been gathered at high cost during the flood.

Guruji sprang up with anger and flew with one jump to the other side; in no time He freed all horses from their loads and chased them away.

The dealer interfered: "Yes, Baba, the wood will go, I

have taken the business; from one Sadhu we took all
the wood and he did not say anything."
That was too much! "Did not say anything? You
haven't seen a Sadhu up to now" Guruji said, and
then the strength of thousand horses came over Him
from the injustice done to a Sadhu. He picked up big
limbs like sticks and threw them at the dealer and his
gang. It was God's will that nobody got killed. They
fell and ran away, the dealer did not even have the
courage to pick up his cycle parked on the island.
A powerful storm and a satisfying peace afterwards.

Guruji's anger had always been against injustice,
ego, pride, and unfaithfulness.
A holy anger full of beauty and grace, a fight from
the deepest corner of His being for truth.
The same energy that empowers the mother to lift
up the truck that has run over her child.
It appeared that almost nobody ever understood
Guruji's anger, besides you, naturally. The disciple,
through the grace of faith, can believe completely in
what the Guru is doing. Never questioning right or
wrong. A Guru is the God manifested; He says the
sun is blue, so it will be blue – what you do not
understand today, maybe tomorrow. That is not the
question – you have to have two hundred percent
faith, whatever might happen.

A thousand and one stories can be told from one
who is constantly in the divine presence,
Sometimes in the form of Shiva or Ram or Krishna or

SIX

Dust Under His Lotus Feet

Your bhakti is at a stage that you love to be the dust under His lotus feet.
Your demonical nature should be smashed under the divine power.
No sacrifice seems to be high enough to manifest your love.
If Guruji were to tell you to jump into the water or cut away any part of your body or the whole,
By God's grace you would be able to fulfill it.
Guruji's love and compassion have always been stronger than His desire or necessity to destroy your sinful, unavoidable presence.
Sometimes Guruji left you in anger, being unable to bear the limitations of mortal existence anymore.
Unable to follow or find a gesture of repentance, you would sink into Ganga Mata's lap and pray for help;
Or you would just keep standing under a tree, eyes and heart in tears and broken, immoveable, no word, no food, no breath, if possible,
Until Guruji's grace turned back.
The night passed the day, the people would stop and try to change your determination to stand and suffer for the rest of your life.

Ganga Maya or Mahamaya[48].
All the heavenly and worldly forms, are they not all the manifestation of the Supreme?

Never Annoy a Saint!
One strange rainy winter night where owls cried loudly and the bats flew around, Guruji must have felt that something odd was going to happen.
"The foreign girl in my care hasn't eaten the whole day; it looks like no food will come from Ganga, so why not make a piece of bread from the rough flour used for the cows."
Smiling, and in full Santosh, the strange bread was put into the fire and when ready, broken into pieces to be eaten.
Strange "guests" appeared.
Not taking off their shoes, or showing any kind of respect, their leader stood with both his arms resting in the tree and talked rudely to Guruji.
"Why are you hanging your arms up like an elephant?" Guruji said annoyed,
"No kind of greeting, no Sitaram, no Radhe Shyam."
"Hey, Baba, take care what you are saying, beggar from nowhere, or we will bind you on a piece of wood and throw you into the Ganga."
Guruji unimpressed as usual replied: "God knows who will be thrown in the Ganga first."
"Alright, let's see tomorrow."
Somehow Guruji's Maya made them disappear in the darkness of the night.

---

[48] The Great Illusion, Lakshmi, the Goddess Herself.

The tension and bad omens still remained in the air.
The little hunger that might have risen fell flat again.
Guruji, without commentary, told you to go to sleep.
Guruji put the fire on, fully alert and fixed His lotus
position and sat in meditation for the rest of the
night. The four o'clock puja call – "Ganga Hare,
Narmade Hare, Hare Mahadev" – rang out over the
Ganga and the nearby area of Haridwar.
The cry of a simple fakir in danger, having no other
weapon against all the violence of the world other
than His unshakable faith and purity of heart.
Naked against a host of enemies, but one with God.
A silent morning meditation was finishing before
sunrise when the news came that the body of the
criminal who visited us in the night had been found
dead in a dry riverbank of the Ganga, smashed to
death by Ganga stones, recognizable only by the ring
on his hand.
OM Shanti.

Similar events happened when persons like police
officers, etc. tried to bother Guruji for having a
foreign girl stay at His place, or demanding valuables
or money, which Guruji didn't have.
By Guruji's Maya, the people received transfer orders
to other places, before they could interfere more in
Guruji's life.
One time the wife of the CID[49] inspector became
jealous of your youth, happiness, and health. "Babaji

---

[49] Foreign Registration Police

what are you feeding to the girl that she is looking so
bright?"
The next day she took her bath in the Ganga, when
Ganga Mata loosened both of her golden earrings.
"Babaji, what have you done, my earrings are gone!"
Most worldly people, not being devotees, are
unaware of the consequences of annoying a Saint or
interfering in His pure living, free from attachment,
desire, or aversion.

But such a bliss of tapasya[50] had not been in your
destiny.
Guruji's mother Lila[51] soon calmed His anger; coming
back He terminated His child's hardships.
Sacrifice is visible devotion and melts away all sins
and faults.
The love of the Gopis: their heights of devotion
reached madness when Krishna disappeared and left
them fallen into separateness and darkness.

In the first phase of the Guru school, you had been
strong to survive all kinds of hardships.
Your reservoir of worldliness proved quite
unshakable.

Divine Anger
What an inconceivable happiness is coming over you,
by passing tests of your belief.
Your own Self is your friend, but also your foe.
Guruji's anger is against your lower nature, which
has been your own enemy as well. Guru and disciple
together are fighting against the same enemy of
pride, ego, or other tamasic energies.
Guruji, out of compassion, and in order to deliver you
from the "rotten tooth" (bad habits) takes the
uncomfortable role of a surgeon or jailor.
Suffering Himself even more than you for the pain
induced. But His love is so boundless, that at any

---

[50] Austerities, repentance performed with the aim of purification
of mind and body..
[51] Mahamaya, Ganga Mata, Lila all refer to the Mother Herself.
Lila means the divine play.

price the poison, your tamas, has to be cut out.
Most of the people, even so-called disciples, run
away after the first angry attacks on their faults.
The ego always wants comfort and honor and
pleasing words.
Therefore it is said in India, the Guru's stick (anger)
is the Guru's blessing.
You understand this.

Suffering as Teaching
After the basic loving relationship, Guruji shows
anger, because you are a form of Maya.
Constantly fighting against it, always trying to be
saved from the snares of Maya.
He tries, with all means, to chase your physical
presence away.
What to do? Ganga Mata's Maya has placed a seed
of truth within you, unfailing faith and love for your
Guru so that your master could cut you to pieces, but
nothing in the world could make you go away or
leave what for you meant heaven.
For purification, all sufferings and hardships turn into
a teaching.

You understand that most of the fakirs manifest a
tamasic way of expression. (For example: an
inconvenient, frightening appearance including naked
and covered with ashes, matted hair, sculls around
the neck, consuming poison, and preparing food with
the wood from crematory grounds.)
All in order to find the truth of the unmanifested soul

behind the form.

Sometimes Guruji shows a very pleasant, loving form, constantly telling how good and beautiful you are, how much your efforts are bearing fruits, etc.

You listen to this, accepting it without agreement.

Lovingly, you would prefer Guruji's anger and humiliations.

What a purification takes place when your ego gets beaten down!

A vanishing ego is half liberation.

How much your love and longing for God's grace grows when Guruji shows His punishing form.

What is it, what do you want, when you become a disciple: only to strengthen your relation with the divine and nothing, nothing else.

Sometimes Guruji is obvious in His contempt for the whole of your being: your past, your present condition, being impure, hopeless, doubtful, weak in your determination.

In front of God, one is always imperfect.

Sometimes you decide to sit in the Ganga water for purification until Guruji's grace calls you back.

How sweet His words, how positive for you, not the least touch of anger, giving up all sufferings and heart tears, flying, weeping of love, back into His shelter.

The Shorter, Harder Path
Soon Guruji's intense work to cut the stone into the

diamond, took not the long and comfortable way, but the harder short cut, even at the risk of losing or ruining you completely.

As much faith as you were able to live, so too Guruji's faith must have been strong in His disciple's determination for truth, though it may cost your life. Often, when teaching power came over Him, to destroy the ego and other obstacles on the path, Guruji felt exhausted and compassionate that He had to act in the way He did, to purify your form of Maya. Still full of Santosh: not He Himself was acting, but only the divine will, or Ganga Mata's Maya through Him.

"We are all Ganga Mata's disciples" He would say. "She creates disciples and She creates the Guru."

Guruji's training was hard and successful.
In a few months the worldly frame of your body started trembling, and your ego, pride, and self-confidence lost ground.
The whole physical and mental statue became porous.
In not more than one year it was ready to be pulled down completely, which meant you were physically and mentally ready to die:
Prepared to give up the body, without losing the immortality of the soul.

The austere living on the island, the rare food once a day, the two pieces of cloth throughout the year in cold, heat, rain,

Did quick destruction to the more or less luxurious
body of a twenty-five year old girl who had been
used to all kinds of tastes and comforts.
There had been many chances to survive: Ganga
Mata provided enough to keep you alive but the
desire for renunciation made you refuse even the
little food there was.
The dream of the beginner to starve for God!
How painful it must have been for your Guru Mother
if the milk, gotten with so many difficulties, was
thrown away by Her child who thought to become a
yogi.
Many a time Ganga Mata sent beautiful sweets; but
the more delicious and expensive it was, the more
you hated and rejected it.
"You didn't come to India to eat cake and apples.
If you like things like this, you can always go back to
Germany" you convinced yourself.

Most of the time you had been so hungry or dried
out, that if, finally, Ganga Mata made some food
possible, you could not eat anymore, it was too late.
Eating or drinking in the open, surrounded by
animals and people who perhaps had none, you
could only give your meal away to a cow or a hungry
dog, or throw your tea into the Ganga, and run into
the jungle to meditate and weep under the next tree.

Like this your body broke up more and more;
The constant diarrhea worked wonders toward this,
with the effect that your sensibility and spirituality

immensely increased.

Suffering is Purification
The rest of ego consciousness was washed away by
the long weeping for nothing:
Feelings of impurity, aloofness, incapability, and
guilt.
You remember days when you just disappeared into
nowhere and nothingness, into the stony dry desert
on the other side of the Ganga.
Going far to weep your heart away for hours in the
heat and stones.
To weep and weep and wash your sinful existence
away.
Not real sadness, the bliss of God's presence or
invisibility was never lost, only purification or utmost
suffering for God.
After a long weeping day like this, in the evening
when you came back, the people on the way would
say: "Now she has become completely crazy."
A body was walking, but empty of anything, all ego-
ness was swept away.
Suffering is purification.

Guruji saw you coming, swaying between heaven
and earth, based in Santosh, self-sufficiency, in
absolute commitment to the divine will. "Will she be
strong enough to hold on the path, to survive for the
divine? Will her karma suppress the determination?
What will happen if she dies somewhere in the
jungle? The police will come and search for the fakir

whose teaching starved the girl to death."

Fakir Forever
Again arose Guruji's impulse to get rid of it all: had
He become a fakir to fall into another responsibility?
Still the one who sacrifices for liberation should be
protected and given a chance.
Ganga Mata will help and lead all for the good.

Guruji's love for God was outstanding: so much
happiness and enthusiasm. Meditation and
austerities were done out of happiness and freedom.
For life and lives He asked to stay a fakir: in sacrifice
of the body and all the riches of the world.
How much you adored this spiritual freedom and
surrender.
Unfortunately your presence, with all the
corresponding responsibilities and natural
involvements,
("If one puts wood on fire, it has to burn"),
All these unavoidable circumstances, seemed to
make it impossible to hold a free fakir life.
We both surrendered to the divine will.
Nothing was more painful for you when Guruji
insulted you: "What you want here, go away, you are
spoiling our innocent free sadhu life."
Then you really wanted to destroy yourself.
But you were made to be there at that very place to
find the Truth.
You prayed to God to give you the strength to
destroy your female face and body in order not to

interfere with Guruji's austerity.

What a miserable condition you had to accept: to be harmful and a disturbance for your most beloved god-like Saint.

How to hide from your own existence.

Ganga Mata, Lord Shiva showed compassion.

Your ignorance was turned into faith, unshakable faith into destiny, the divine will, and your karma.

"Don't worry, paradise is near, some more tests, and time will heal."

Above all, what is time, this earthly bondage will pass by or change into a divine play.

Guruji always lived complete Santosh and finally accepted our Guru-disciple relationship.

Your daily prayer: "God is your everything: mother, father, friend, and husband."

Unconditionally, without exceptions.

Silent meditations called into the night for a solution. Silence of truth, absence of thought, too empty, too weak to desire anything, not even liberation.

Surrender

Time goes on and, by itself, stiffness has to bend without being broken.

In the winter the fire became our blanket, the cows our shelter.

If there was a blanket, it happened that the cows would eat half in the night, which again would raise Guruji's anger. He would wake us in the night. "A yogi," He said "should sleep like a dog, always awake

in conscious sleep."
Guruji almost never slept, alert in lotus position,
sitting by the fire with the Ganga and her holy song
of Her Lord's name:
Hare Hare Hare.

You were trained to get up every hour in the night.
"There is a cow behind the tent." "Bring a glass of
water." "Put some wood on the fire."
Wonderful, you never remembered a deep sleep for
more than three hours.
Always outdoors, so sleeping during the day was
forbidden.
You agreed that laziness is the biggest obstacle on
the spiritual path.
Out of fear, you tried to never fall into deep sleep.
How angry He became when His three or four o'clock
conch was blown after another Sadhu had surprised
us with his early puja[52].
Guruji loved to be the first one to worship the Ganga,
Shiva, and the Gods in the morning.
Wake up, bath, meditation, worship, whatever time it
might be.

Surrender completely to the will of Ganga's Maya and
the result of former karma.
"We have been together for many lifetimes."
Clearer and clearer you saw this holy relation:

---

[52] Worship of the Divine through invocations, prayers, songs, and
rituals.

each life you had been struggling to get free from
human bondage to reach divine liberation.
This life should be the last: all unattached relations
and austerity, not avoiding obligatory duty.
Guruji always said: "Whatever you have to suffer,
live it out in this life."
Sometimes everything was tainted by the worldly
explanation
Of karma, good and bad.
On the path to liberation every choice and action is
cleared by the understanding of its heavenly origin.
Guruji, who always appeared to you as an attendant
of Lord Shiva, or even as the Lord Shiva himself in a
reduced form, might have been cursed to live in a
human relationship, to experience its limitations, and
at this time using His divine origin to give liberation
to His consort-disciple.

Time passed nicely for Guruji as a Shiva Sadhu,
enjoying some of the world's so-called pleasures.
On the other side, Guruji, unattached to the world,
often mentioned that whatever He did was "just for
you," such as staying near the town of Haridwar,
instead of in a cave in the Himalayas.
"How could you have found me, if I resided in the
high mountains?"
Or if there would be a Bandhara[53]: "You still need a
lot of food and facilities, otherwise you will die before
you get liberation."

---

[53] Celebration

Words of truth you listened to with humiliation and shame.
But what to do, one cannot just jump to the top of the mountain.
You had been blessed by all this renunciation, and remembered that all devotion, understanding, and austerities you received through His grace only.
Guruji wanted you to be true to yourself according to the faith of your life – no sin, no honor.
Whatever hidden corner in your mind might contain a dream, a desire to be fulfilled: it had to come out and be lived out.
Life in service to the divine will.
Learning all the time, experiencing for higher renouncement, purifying for realization.
Santosh had been the name of Guruji and His teachings.
You demonstrated contentment in living, not with the pleasant and agreeable, but with acceptance of what was contrary to your preferences.
The divine play was enveloped in a form of bliss: the curse of karma became acceptable as a beneficial gift.

Guruji never renounced anything, being manifested renouncement Himself. "No grasping, no abandoning."
Austerities were not an achievement, not even really austerities.
Being a Sadhu from His very being, and living truthfulness, no force or suppression were necessary.

Even accepting Maya and emotion, His mind never fell into the traps of attachment, because He was truly connected with Brahman, the one without a second.

Maya as Brahman's sport, both a manifestation and its exaltation.

Siddhis Belong to God

Guruji had always been a Siddha[54] of the modest invisible kind.

His siddhis seemed to be natural occurrences: was it a miracle or just a perfect coincidence of happening? Guruji used to say that whatever occurred was only Ganga Mata's siddhi.

Jesus never thought Himself curing the sick, or that it was Him who made the lame walk and the dead alive – it was simply the grace of the Father, fulfilling His Son's wish.

By surrendering fully to the divine will, whatever the Saint would like to have happen would be fulfilled, because of His oneness with the Supreme Self.

Guruji usually preferred to hide any kind of divine energy or knowledge of medicine, or of the past or future.

If somebody dared to ask to see His siddhis, Guruji would certainly have thrown him out of the ashram. The one who flies in the air is not a Yogi; the Yogi who knows, does not fly.

Somebody challenged: "Babaji look, there is a cow,

---

[54] A Siddha is a perfected being who also has special powers or abilities: siddhis.

struggling in the middle of the Ganga. Baba throw a mantra that it turns to the bank."

Guruji, uninterested, said: "No need, the Ganga will save it." And lo, Guruji had not finished talking, and the calf turned to the bank where some people helped it out and it ran away.

Guruji just loved to be nobody and nothing – no family, no wealth, no knowledge, no education.
Sitting in meditation during the night, when nobody was awake.
Blowing the puja conch at three a.m. when everybody was asleep and resting when everybody was awake, playing the family man and farmer, serving the cows or playing cards, or by showing an angry, uncomfortable being.

Die One Hundred Times
Even Guruji wondered at the lack of any sign of injury, from the punishments for His child's ego and pride, though sometimes He even threw burning wood on her.
One time His anger against Maya in the form of yourself grew over the danger line. He knew no way to help other than, with a strength from above, to lift your whole body up and throw you some distance away.
That had been too much even for the faithful devotees around: they decided to leave Guruji and moved under the next tree to sit silently in a circle and decide how to handle Guruji's anger.

Even you thought that this had been the end of your
physical existence.
However, always understanding and agreeing with
Guruji's treatment: what to do with such a stubborn
form of Maya? Better to smash it all down and start
again with a new body.

Nature is changing, immortality is not so easy to
achieve – you die a hundred times and still your ego
survives.
Maybe even God becomes tired and gives up
transforming you into a diamond, considering
whether or not to give liberation in the very
incomplete form you are in.
Guruji was digging deep into your unconscious to
catch the last invisible trace of the monster: the
hidden ego.
Yes, by Ganga Mata's grace, you could stand on
Guruji's side to kill the enemy, enjoying the grace of
right understanding.

Guruji never taught obviously.
Only the one of complete faith is able to see that
Guruji's mere presence is a teaching.
Every breath gives you divine consciousness,
You feel that you are protected by His being in each
and every moment.
Divine love – the all-pervading Almighty – the
Universal Being. Your individuality is only a part of it,
Cosmic energy in which nature and supreme spirit
are miraculously interwoven.

You have to learn that Guru and disciple are one, like
the mother and the child.
The first teaching on the spiritual path: you are not
the doer. Whatever is happening within body and
mind is the will of your Guru.

Every night the same struggle: fight against laziness,
heaviness, distraction, the pride to become
enlightened.
The goddess mantra has to be called a thousand
times to help to win over the enemies.
Guru meditation shall help to get the child trained for
immortality from human bondage
No divinity is spared, no religion left out.
With spirits all around, your grossness makes you
blind and lame and mentally retarded.
All your efforts dissolve in the alluring tricks of the
mind to live in the golden middle way:
Another sleep, another consolation.
Every few hours you wake up: another try, and jump
to embrace the divine nectar holding it for a second,
and then weakness and mortality make you slip
down again into another next morning rebirth.
Is the God/Guru letting you hang and struggle like
the fish out of the water?
As much as you want the bliss of water, this desire
will never be enough for now:
Karma, blindness, and inertness are still in power.
In moments of light there is patience, smile,
dissolution of all into all.
God doesn't feed sweets to His beloved child more

than once in an endless time.
Meditation happens when you give up the will;
To sit in your true nature is not to be achieved as
something from outside.

One night you will be awakened to know of sleep
and awareness,
Will walk without movement between illusion and
reality, one interweaving with the other.
Still sitting on the ground, you will be gone far away,
Long ago.
The voice is telling a story of now, while singing to
the flute behind the clouds.
Watching the many of this and that, with eyes that
belong to the final vision.

The veil of illusion is mystical enough, that you even
do not know that is was lifted long ago.
You smile and embrace the Divine as your own Self,
Surrender and dissolve, to die to live immortal.

Guru and Ganga
Shiv Shiv Shiv
Along the banks of the Ganga are places charged
with thousands of years of meditative energy, such
as Haridwar and Rishikesh.
The vibration becomes so strong, that your own little
limited being starts transforming into the spirit and
renunciation of the ancient Rishis.
Endless times of meditation or dissolving into your
divine dream.

Your happiness is residing in the Self; the world is
full of hardships and poorness, but God's love,
Guruji, and Gangaji are present beyond the form in
the smile of truth, being manifested through your
devotion, incomparable to all the treasures of this
world.
Life has become truthful, a deep, deep thanksgiving
in which the giver, the gift, and the receiver have
become one.
Such a familiarity, a oneness, with all the children of
God.

The world blames and humiliates, but Saints, your
ancient fathers of lifetimes past, only embrace you
and forgive your impurities.
The all-understanding Ones: finally you have found a
way to reach their subtleness.
Such comfort when your soul finds its original home,
to know it will never leave you again, however big
the obstacle to overcome appears to be.
Guruji's family, the Saints of renunciation, fill one
heaven by themselves, wild and shining Nagas, the
orange Swamis, never forgetting their former fakir
life of ash and nakedness.

Guruji's mission has been continuously, solemnly,
Shiv, Shiv, Shiv.
No more, no less.
The answer to all questions is the lotus position, the
eyes closing to the Infinite and a soundless voice,
stronger than all the silence.

No expression, all experienced as eternally
understood.
All the universities, the disputes, and lectures
dissolve in the simplicity of the final truth: Shiv Shiv
Shiv.
For this bliss, less than a moment, able to overtake
all your life, for this invisible Shiv,
One has renounced all the knowledge of the western
past,
Has abandoned country, culture, family, and friends,
Has given up the occupation that defined you a long
time ago.
How easy, so incredibly easy: once having been
chosen for the Light, who cares about the darkness,
whose unsurpassable reality has been the ignorance
of your life.
"Shiv Shiv Shiv," balm for the ailing heart of
generations – one smile, like the sun and moonlight,
when the clouds are dispelled.

Guruji knows all, but doesn't tell – no words –
Your love and faith are unshakable.
The book of life has to be learned on this little island
spot. The black and white pages, the rotten and the
glamorous ones, all has to happen on the same
island stage, just for you, to make you understand
micro cosmos and macro cosmos, the same prana[55]
in truth and falsehood.
Guruji and Ganga Mata seem to work perfectly

---

[55] Universal life energy, the life force that infuses all beings, all
manifestation.

together to open a drama, Lila, in all shades: from
cruelty to blessing, from emotions to detachment,
both grotesque and obscure, - just to teach your little
heart not to run away in fear or doubt.

Love for your Guru, love for Ganga Mata.
The tests become harder and harder, your strength
is failing, but God's grace doesn't lose the grip of His
hand.
Trust that He will never let you fall to perish.
Your courage is His compassion – somehow you pass
in spite of all the failures. Whatever happens, the
immortal tiny "Shiv Shiv Shiv" is there,
Shining, even when the whole worldly building
crashes over you.
From outside actually nothing happens, you just
squat under the tree or by the Ganga stones and
watch your inside, bursting and churning around.
No father, no mother, no friend, no knowledge, not
anything, but you are mother, father, relations,
wealth, knowledge, ...everything.

All has to be understood without a lecture, without a
book, without advice.
Nature, people, movements, and decay – to leave it
and become immune to its tricks, to renounce the
world – why not before God's glory?
But do you not renounce His brilliance together with
His manifestations?
What remains? Is not the seed inseparable from the
tree it contains?

"Questions are not allowed." Guruji says one time when you dare to ask "Why?"
"Do you want to quarrel with God?"
Once and forever you sink back into silence with yourself.
You have to be solid and unshakable, like a rock on which God can rely.
Anger, hardships, suffering, deep pain, weakness, dying, aloneness, and emptiness, all are leading you down into the dreadful dungeon.
But there on the ground of your inner being, God's smile is awaiting you, embracing you unconditionally.

Ten Years
A full ten years of renouncement on the island under the trees, surrounded by the waves of love of Mother Ganga.
No books, no memory, no other valuables than the universal prana inside.
No other Lord to be worshipped than the mantra of Shiva transforming into the All, all around.
Guru is Shiva, Ganga is Shiva, sun is Shiva, your mind is Shiva, the blessings and hardships are Shiva.
Shiva in your eyes, Shiva in your hands, Shiva in your ears.
Shiva is your dream, Shiva is the past, Shiva is your death.

Ten years pass in Shiv; on the screen of Shiv all the many colorful and opposing events, the ups and downs, happen on this universal substratum of Shiva.

Like the tree unshakable, grounded in its origin, a
new life has grown ahead, on its own, yet still a part
of the whole.
Alak Niranjan: God the Separate One.
How strong you are in the Oneness with Shiva, all
alone in the Truth of the all.
Guruji's yogic presence was a presence of the
invisible, the untouchable – just like your heart and
soul inside.

Ten years of Guru, Ganga, cows, and wandering in
the jungle,
Shiv Shiv Shiv.
Life, whose only support is faith, devotion, austerity,
and determination to truth – may it cost your
miserable life.

Ten years, the fire and its ash to concentrate on, the
waves of the Ganga surround you, whispering and
murmuring the inexpressible, to listen to for hours,
days, and years.
You cannot understand, still you know.
The loving waves of the water, the happy and weird
bird in the air, the passing living people, melt into
one with the dead bodies floating down the river.
You sit and witness, searching the unity of inside and
outside.

Nature, for a certain time, holds its shape;
Beauty, purity, the renouncement, the discipline.
The law of nature is change: the most perfect spring

time wants to give up its pleasantness and is
tempted by the fullness, the over-ripeness of the
perfect summertime.
What an ecstasy to become intoxicated by the
summer night swinging its scent-loaded wind.
The fruit ripens to excess and you have to smash it
down, suffering the spreading smell – the reaction of
your enjoyment.
The cause is quickly accepted but the consequences
are long and troublesome, never ending,
What a waste of time to suffer the reaction!
If you had known – would you have been able to
avoid the cause?
Maybe – maybe not.

The winter of asceticism.
The renouncement of the blossom of nature, for the
truth hidden under the surface, is the real bliss of
your life.
How much sincerity there has been in starving or
freezing for the divine.
Such pure happiness in not eating the gifts of the
world, in not accepting their nets and traps that spin
around you the temptation of luxury – only to pull
you deeper down in illusion.
How painful it is when Guruji's anger strikes you,
Nevertheless it is an embrace of truth and
compassion,
Sweeter than Maya's passion.

Spring changes nature,

Winter leads to death,
The will to survive is the law,
The buds are still alive and able to sprout.

Does God also become emotional?
Guruji could not bear anymore the suffering of His
child for Truth,
Its willingness to die, even before enlightenment.
Maya is strong, your determination to die for the soul
is weak and without the support of the body.
Nature is an expression of the Supreme,
Its perfect reflection.
Learn to accept,
To overcome, and survive, for the Truth.

SEVEN

The Web of Maya Spreads

Temptations of Maya
The play of Maya announces herself on the traditional festival of Divali, the celebration of the Goddess Lakshmi, Mahamaya.
Divali is celebrated in November, when the days are bright and promising but the nights are cold.
The first blow of Maya arrives to our ascetic island paradise when a Maya-Sadhu builds a hut of bamboo by our fireplace, full of pride and pretending protection.
Guruji and you, His disciple child, squat at the fire by the cows, worshipping Lakshmi Devi from the depths of the heart through renouncement of any brilliance or temptation of Maya.
Our sincere devotion closes the senses.
Not the least attraction for any improvement of our life, blessed by Ganga Mata, cow Mata, the fire and the endless soundless song of "OM Namah Shivaya" shining from inside brighter than all the thousands of Divali lights.

Wonderful, unforgettable, all ego-body is destroyed, no strength to show any sign of pleasure or distress, of cold or warm, the pure land behind the smile and the tears.

The world and a movement, even God and the
Goddess, dissolve into a blissful nothingness.
The bottom of life is reached, where life and death
embrace themselves to dissolve.

Before your physical existence fades away, Maya
calls you back to life, to take part in the holy game
once more.
Another round, like waking up every morning for
another attempt to conquer the invincible Maya.

The second temptation of Maya is more successful:
"Lakshmi Devi" arrives in a very clever form, sure not
to be chased away.
A van full of treasures appears, carrying your sister,
her friend, and her five year old son. "Narvadaji,
your sister." Guruji says calmly, being used to the
divine play.
No reaction is possible from your side.
Too long since your mouth has smiled, your voice
has talked, your arms have embraced.
Just watching the dream going on.
No responsibility on your part, to fulfill anybody's
expectations.

An unworldly condition really: your sister travels ten
thousand miles to arrive in the far east, Baba Guruji
doesn't know any word of English or communication,
and the little sister without any sign of life, sticks in
the grey of ash, demonstrating the promised heaven
of bliss and truth.

Guruji as usual understands and doesn't scold.
Our voyage to the sources has reached its end of
grayness,
Maya has to come and help to get you out of the
dead-end.
This is not final liberation: revive and learn to smile
again.
What is the use of finding the jewel on the bottom of
the lake – does not the jewel want to be brought up
to show its brilliance of heavenly truth?
Guruji's Maya met Ganga's motherly care: their child
will learn to laugh again.
As long it took to tear down the disciple's body of
illusion, as long it might take to restore the purified
image of the unavoidable karma.
One will stick to the truth, whatever has to be lived
out will be done, passed, and survived.
No shame: the aim is clear, the Saints are all
compassion, acceptance will be already liberation.

A New Birth
The next morning, the unavoidable dawn of a change
comes and starts the beginning of a Maya
adjustment, which seems to impose itself, possibly
for the rest of your life.
If you don't die to be liberated, then the alternative
lies in being in the world.
The sentiments of the older sister are strong and not
so easy to ignore.
The love and gifts are simple and normal but how
and why to explain that ordinary human relations

and conversation have become ridiculous and unbearable.

The first days you are strong enough to refuse, but Maya's honey works patiently and confidently.

Slowly the physical cracks and wounds all over your body are felt and cured.

With the recovering of injuries come the first smiles. Life has won and Maya goes on.

A pilgrimage to Krishna's birthplace, Vrindabhan, and Girnar, the mystical seat of the god Dattatreya[56], the Taj Mahal, Jaipur, and Pushkar.

Powerful attractions; helplessly you swim forward in Guruji's Maya stream.

Guruji Himself finds the acceptance of Ganga Mata's "blessing" not un-dangerous.

Can this be a wish-fulfilling boon, meeting the manifestation of Mother Ganga, yet still preserving one's fakir life?

For all renunciates, a not so easy task.

The child comes naked and innocent still carrying a whole world of temptations and potentials inside.

In earlier renunciations, temptations of Maya were absent.

You are unable to refuse divine conception: together with Guruji you have to sit in the mini-bus and drive from town to town, from goods things to bad. You have become the cause of this immense powerful new flow of Maya.

---

[56] One of the twenty-four incarnations of Vishnu, a deity with three heads symbolizing Brahma, Vishnu, and Shiva.

Guruji smiles the eternal acceptance, but the pure
heart of the born ascetic starts revolting, defending
its simplicity and truthfulness.
Guruji finds Himself serenely seated on silk and
brocade and is made to take His food on exotic silver
plates with decorated spoons.
Guruji's jungle beauty is exposed to laughing crowds
of masked humans.
The Maharaja of the Ganga island,
where all wishes are fulfilled without the help of
Maya's greatest trap – money,
Now has to make money a servant, being constantly
confronted with, and dependent on, its presence.
Poor Guruji, how honestly and courageously He
protects His innocence!
How far away the heavenly island has gone, lost in
deserts of stones and desires.

Maya will take us on the trials of pilgrimage from the
gate of heaven "Haridwar," over Indraprast (Delhi) to
the Taj Mahal, and finally the first recovering in
Krishna's kingdom: Mathura-Vrindabhan.
Krishna's presence is able to replace Ganga Mata's
protection.
Maya's dreamland passes by, no time anymore to
dissolve yourself in the waves of your own weakness.
Has paradise been lost or have you to learn its
transformation?
To learn, you need strength, physically and mentally.
Your body in Guruji's school of renouncement has
learned to give up and die for the bliss of the Atman.

Now in the world there is nothing useful left: your
blood has become water, your bone like rubber,
while walking the legs collapse, a loud word of any
worldly kind hits like a sword and makes you shed
tears of blood.

The heavenly ecstasy of the island has changed into
a painful carrying of an unbearable bodily burden.
Death becomes more and more urgent.
Life is impossible to live; God's Maya, unacceptable.
Certainly the bliss of the soul and God's presence has
always been indestructible reality.
What is the soul without the dressing of the body?
A solution cries to be found: death, a transformation
from one faith to another.

Guruji by your side – His sweet love sheds tears in
your heart.
Your Guru suffers with you, you being the cruel form
and the cause of suffering.
We are going to Girnar, the seat of Guru Dattatreya.
Yes, God is victory over death.
Hold on to your faith and life is near again: the next
life after passing another death.

Your body energy has slowly grown into your long
matted hair,
Jattas[57], the sign of austerity, manifested energy.
Austerities have an end, changing into an advanced

---

[57] Matted hair, dreadlocks.

beginning.

On Christmas, one day before starting the pilgrimage
to Lord Dattatreya, Guruji, with His own hands,
finally takes the last step and shaves His child,
cutting the hair tuff for initiation into Sannyas.
Everything had been taught and tested before,
The shaving ceremony had never been necessary.
The two cloths, the rudraksh[58] mala, and the mantra,
are your only possessions[59] and will protect you for
the rest of your life.

The new birth begins.
New enthusiasm to live God's devotion and serve.
The dream of austerities is not gone, but you can
only live what is presented to you, bright or grey,
strong or withering.
The pilgrimage to Lord Dattatreya becomes the
happiest days of your new life.
Passing the steps of the ten thousand floods your
new birth with a previously unknown purity of love,
fun, and excitement.
Forward and back you run, like the child who can't
wait to arrive at the top, nor can understand why the
elders are delaying to reach the goal.
Nothing extraordinarily divine happens.

---

[58] The seed of the holy Rudraksh Tree used in initiation to
Sannyas; believed to the be tears of Shiva.
[59] Sannyasis may have no stitched clothes; at "birth" (i.e.:
initiation) they are given only one cloth to wrap lower body and
one to wrap shoulders. They are also given a mala (rosary,
prayer beads), here made from rudraksh seeds.

Just the immense natural simplicity and innocence
through which God's presence and grace are
manifesting itself.
Enlightened infants don't know of the separate one,
only the one, the one without a second.

Since this dance of bliss at Girnar, bodily or mental
kinds of diseases are no more able to touch you.
Worldly and spiritual life become inseparable, fully
accepted, content to live to the end.
The caterpillar's transformation is finished – no
matter whether superior or inferior, silk is to be
produced.

OM Guruji!
Your child grew up and survived its serious tears,
fully established in God and Guruji's will.
The life that is supposed to follow is tainted by an
unavoidable game of Maya.
Not visible at once, but an uncooked seed was
planted and most probably meant to sprout.
Hari OM tat Sat.

Part Two: Catharsis

ONE

Seeds Sprout and Grow

Another Test ... Another Proof
One seems to be always astonished how things could happen and sprout to such an extent.
Nevertheless the seed had been set unknown times ago – too late to grieve, too early to rejoice.
OM Guruji.

The path of awakening – started in austerities – had shown glimpses of fulfilling the promises.
Where had the courage and fearless faith led?
Never asking to reach a goal –
Guruji had chosen the path of deviation:
Back and forth
In purification of parabdha karma[60].
God's garden of paradise is always beautiful, may it even be from the near outside.
Leading your dreams back into the very depth of the world:
Marriage!
A dream most unwanted for a spiritual aspirant.

The grace shown to you cannot allow any demand or wish.

---

[60] Accumulated past actions, the fruits of which are experienced now and cannot be erased.

Was not all spirituality and desire for renouncement
presented to you by His compassion?
"Straw will catch fire when put above burning wood."
"Choose me and abandon your newborn vow of
celibacy or go away and starve to death in the cave
of your dreamed austerity."
Guruji's eyes are glowing like the fire flames,
Mother Ganga flows by all smiling;
The divine Lila takes place.
The play of consciousness cannot become impure or
uncontrolled.
Never had there been a question, a doubt, or
weakness:
You had already given everything.
Had anything ever belonged to you?
Another test – another proof.
Guruji's love would be always with you in a worldly
life of high love, but lower quality, or in heavenly
abodes of purified limitations.
How can you reach and enjoy the "high" without
appreciating the "low?"
Ram will be born one day -
Rejoice and delay your yogic dreams.
If the spirit of meditation falls into manifestation,
The fall into illusion seems to be unavoidable.
Guru's grace had given you unshakable faith, if not
the final liberation through meditation.
The path goes on,
Passing into an unavoidable setback:
Had this disciple been incapable of a higher solution?
So it is as it was and such is the beneficial.

High peaks of meditation drown
Guruji's Shiva-like divinity, capturing it into human
limitation.
Your inner sense is not able to save the immortality
of the young independent proud Son of God.
OM Guruji.

You curse yourself for falling into the differentiation
of man and woman.
Nevertheless!
Another hindrance of ignorance will be conquered by
time, through acceptance and forbearance.
The question goes on struggling its way from
ignorance to truth:
Had anything been avoidable?
Things happen only because one was unable to
change them.
The past is part of your ignorance.
The now is the wise decision of yesterday.
The childhood faith was learning to read the
scriptures, to become strong in living the truth of a
better decision.
Discrimination!

Guruji didn't like to learn by the mind alone;
The truth should be lived through all the pores of
your bodily and mental life.
Ignorance, weakness, a passion that will have to be
demonstrated, open as the status quo.
Never to hide or suppress the fact is the Truth,
The Law of nature

Immortal Purusha, immortal Prakriti.
The longing for the taste follows the idea of the
flower's beauty.
Why would Ganga Mata's Maya make Him care for
the plant if the fruit is forbidden?
Guruji's inner sense only followed the waves of the
flow –
Including the consequences.
The ever free: had there ever been somebody to
explain or apologize?
Bondage as part of the freedom.
Guruji presented you the key:
Shiva Shiva Shiva
Shiv is truth - all else is false.

How boldly and excitedly you entered the path –
The door sprung open
And in you smiled and danced yourself through the
beginning of paradise,
Knowing little – still offered immortal presence.
Enthusiasm, the direct awareness of grace, could
have made you become unaware of certain dangers
to be avoided – even in heaven.

When spiritual happiness flows over, it has to be held
in a form: in the physical, sensual sign of laughter, a
joke, a direct eye contact.
The manifestations, the shades of heaven and earth
are in no time interwoven.
Its consequences take form – Maya senses
attractions all around, seems to weave the pure

mystical into temptation and the web starts and
sprouts:
The budding fruit cannot be returned into the dream
of the idea.
Things happen:
The fruit that falls cannot be replaced back into the
tree.
One star falls:
The same has changed into another "just like the
same."
The Ganga, the motherly witness, smiles on what
was known long before.
Guru and disciple take refuge back into silent,
separate meditation.
Love for God can never change-
The sacrifice cannot be replaced.
Now you are fallen on the ground.
The song goes on
The sound can differ
The idea remains
Still a change in the same: like the bird's tune on the
height appears as another when placed beneath.
Something is lost
Like the child's smile grows old when grown up.
An adjustment had been accepted.
Guruji's wild beauty put into a cage –
Who will fear a caged lion's growl?

So It Will Be
Years go on. The island of austerity: the Ganga, the
cows and Guruji, your mantra OM Namah Shivaya,

seva, and sacrifice.
All flows forward or deepens into an unknown
establishment of the future.
Faith makes us follow blindly,
Shall it be forever?
Your learning grows higher to understand the
incomprehensible
Law of nature,
The drive of sensuality once in a season has to be
accepted gently as the unavoidable in your fate.
Whoever imagined, that there is austerity in living
sensuality,
Sacrifice in bearing the most beautiful worldly
pleasure,
Pain and sadness in consuming offered fruits.
Spots of karma to be exhausted.
The white dress every girl receives is bound to spoil
itself as life's ways impose the painful experiences of
pleasure.
Nevermore the same innocent whiteness, but God's
compassion will let it shine in the glow of His own
nature.
A deep breath.
No smile of acceptance;
No tears of anger:
God is all, Guruji is great,
Ganga Mata's compassion will lead you safely on the
path of purification.
A cloud to be passed to reach the clear sky of the
void.
No escape.

Live out in *this* life what had been postponed many times.
Now your whole being is made up of faith and divine love:
You surely will survive earthly temptations.
This time not falling into sensuality, but running away from it.
Obligatory works will be burned by the fire of yoga.
The world will misunderstand the desire for liberation, according to its own drive for pleasure.
The holy ones, whose real child you are, recognize your tears of painful attempts.
No words - but compassion - as we are all hanging and dancing this worldly part according to the divine strings and tunes.
Everything is planned so long ago.
"Why do you weep my friend?"

Once when austerity had become unbearable your Maya sister appeared on the island, and turned into a renunciate to heal your wounds and build up your forgotten body again.
Now with your austerity child soon to be born, the all-caring Ganga Mata has to improve the security of Her wild and proud fakir and His girl child and mate:
Your biological mother in old age has to be called to travel all the long way from her German home over wild Turkistan and Afghanistan to establish a place and property for the coming divine children.
The Allahabad Kumbha Mela gives Sannyas to your sister and stamps, through the gentle form of your

all-accepting little mother, the end of the island's
austerity time:
Soon a land will be bought that Guruji had seen in
His dream, a large beautiful playground near the
Ganga, surrounded by jungle, and Saints dwelling in
huts, the already-established Saints in ashrams.

Ganga Mata prepares even before we, the parents,
know about the ones to come.
How gently the web of Mahamaya entangles the
changing condition into a tempting, sensible one.
Let it be – surely – let it be.
You wonder how the soul's imagined call for the
Infinite could be driven into acceptance of illusion.
From adjustment to adjustment,
In spite of all cries towards eternity and sacrifices, to
the best of your understanding,
Maya moves on, inexhaustible source of pleasure,
comfort, and improvements.
No attraction, no temptation -
Guruji's Santosh had built its defense –
We both will go through the narrow worldly path
according to Ganga Mata's surprises.

Your dreadlocks are mounting up again on your
shining body,
Signs of what soon will turn into a past of heavenly
sacrifices.
Your little loving worldly mother comes and has a
right to pray for her daughter's welfare as the world
understands it.

Mothers' sacrifice for their children is too great not to
fulfill unavoidable wishes and settlements: to enjoy
old age by watching the grandchildren grow.
For the price of your austerity, you will have to offer
fulfillment of this last wish of hers in return for the
sleepless nights caused by your proud
renouncement.
The day the future ashram land is registered,
Malaria fever shakes your birth into a new
settlement.
The weight and heat of your dreadlocks becomes
unbearable,
You give up –
They fall –
The Ganga waves swallow them easily.
Maya counts its victories, its defeats.

Still, the settlement into a secure promising world
could not have been more smooth and dream
fulfilling:
A wide land is chosen near the Ganga Islands of the
Seven Rishis, where once you had rambled around in
the ecstasy of your free divine love.
An old banyan tree[61] rejuvenates, times of former
birth, now we meet again in its shadow,
And the children to be born will play with its air
roots.

---

[61] Kind of fig tree, respected as holy, having long air
roots hanging down like the dreadlocks of Lord Shiva.

Building a Shelter

The ruins of this pilgrim shelter space on the old footpath to the abode of the gods (Badrinath, Kedarnath, Gangotri, Yamunotri[62]) will create new rumors into the present to fulfill the unavoidable law of the seed growing into a tree.

Guruji obediently follows the growth of His fierce fire from the tree in the wilderness into the shelter of civilization.

The world will turn the snakes[63] sitting under the stars along the waves of the Ganga into the establishment of an ashram.

"Never make an ashram!"

The warning call of the ascetics!

But Maya will start building.

Keep your renunciation, but the walls will grow around,

Most beautifully adorned with flowers of pride and honor.

Once you enter the kingdom of heaven, from where there is no return,

You swing and swing in the mantra of devotion and faith.

The golden touch turns everything whatsoever into bliss and a necessary presentation of divine grace.

From the island's fire home after the nightly bath and Aarti puja in the early morning dawn, the disciples walk behind Guruji towards a new rising sun.

---

[62] Four pilgrimage places in the Himalayas.
[63] The abandoned ashram site was full of snakes when Babaji first arrived.

Along the Ganga northwards where once the Seven
Rishis sat in meditation,
Arriving to blow the sunrise conch to fulfill God's will.
From all sides helping hands are joining:
Longtime disciples from Guruji's austerity time and
new seekers from abroad passing by.

Your sister enjoys the freedom of a new birth into a
sadhu life as a reward for a long sacrificing service.
She had come six years ago, sent by your mother, to
bring the little adventurer sister back to normal, and
got embraced herself into the divine web of eternity.
Steadily through renouncement she served and won
herself into freedom:
The served ones (her husband, her son, her mother)
abandoned her so that she could struggle her way to
the almost unachievable.
She gave all that there could be to donate, setting
herself thereby into divine nothingness while fixing
for Guruji and His disciples the walls of an ashram
establishment and its unavoidable consequences.

The Call Doesn't Stop
From renouncement to enjoyment, from pleasure to
austerity.
The activity in the ashram left you alone back on the
island-Ganga-home to meditate into Her waves,
dreaming backwards, to stop the future.
First you will have to become an Indian of the Rishi's
heritage,
Or if not yourself, then through the son who will be

born.
Already born months ago under your heart from your
center –
But you don't want to feel and know and accept.
Again you are alone with the godlike miracle.
Your mother left long ago, your sister had gone to
settle the final ashram establishment.
Guru and Ganga Mata's will work on and on, happily,
to grow a garden for the long-known yet unknown
player.
A surprise of youthful happiness to the bewildered
parents.
What has to happen is ready before you accept it.

One afternoon, leaving the island heading toward the
ashram:
What happened?
How did the sign form a new presence?
A playful jump in your inside and you know that you
have become two.
A sweet proceeding and contribution to the
continuity of your little world.
Shiv- Shiv-
The call and love of your past now:
Ganesha[64] – Gaurinanda – the joy of Gauri-Parvati.
Sitting in the rickshaw, the whole world around melts
into a Samadhi[65] not up into the Infinite but right into
the depth of limitation.

---

[64] Elephant-headed God who is the son of Shiva and Parvati-
Gauri
[65] A state of union with God, achieved through meditation.

All melts away, disappears into the bliss of presence,
Before the ego of yours will create obstructions.
An endless ride from the unknown to the sweet
known.

You will carry what belongs to you alone.
It will be shared when the birth will come.
Guruji's sensuality –
Never accepted nor longed for -
Had been placed inside you:
A manifestation of devotion from your side and
compassion from His.
"And if there will be a child?" Guruji once asked.
The mother of us both, Ganga Mata, will know.

For days you walk around alone with your secret.
How to tell a truth of former lives.
With Guruji you never talked of or about something.
"Are you not doing anymore yoga practice?
You are getting heavy."
A flash of lightening!
You smile and run to the banyan tree in the garden
Guruji's understanding makes Him follow.
The divine joy must have filled Him as it had filled
you.
Still, until He reaches your hiding place, His feelings
are gathered together under His normal anger-filled
appearance.
Guruji's time on earth was not to pacify or give
pleasure or enjoyment but to purify, punish,
humiliate, to cut the stone into the diamond,

To transform ego into divine consciousness.
"Maybe you visit your mother and sister ….
Maybe some place in the mountains …"
A weak try for a chance of change from outside.
But the truth already spreads its reality,
A hidden oasis of bliss might be getting surrounded
by worldly impurities of laughter, rumors, and talks,
to pull down a celestial beauty into the mud of
sensuality.

After ten years of accepted austerity, exciting,
shocking news for the misunderstanding ones;
dependency on bodily laws had proved to win over
renouncement and its impossibility.
The wise, the Brahmin, the twice-borns, are
celebrating with flower and brightness, the victory of
Mahamaya to maintain Dharma[66] in this universe.
Tales of the Rishis and their holy heritage are told in
supporting a truth leading back to the primordial
union of Shiva and Shakti:
Pure consciousness and its manifestation,
The coming into being of the universe,
Austerity and sacrifice are the original cause of
whatever will be.

Maya has to be created to move on the universal
wheel of continuity and progeny.
Maya - always passing, never constant, a pleasant
dream, a play inside stiff austerities.

---

[66] Living in accordance with Divine will.

So it is – so it will be.
You see yourself laughing from the one inside who
soon will join the cosmic dance.
Once in a while there comes through that smile that
only mothers can have even while struggling,
starving, fighting, being humiliated.
The determination seems to be missing: how young
mothers are supposed to be to serve creation.
Unable to avoid the hunger for dissolution, your
longing to leave behind –
Everything – without concession.
Renouncement is accepting the unavoidable.
In the holy time of youth you were placed into
freedom, bliss, and faith.
Having tasted the Divine and passed the test that no
worldly enjoyment or temptation can make you
return to the world,
You have to go back and prove how deep your
detachment has advanced or been completed.
In this waiting time you are fully resting in the Divine
– your faith, your love, and your devotion, even the
acceptance of the most powerful root of all
worldliness: parentage.
Still in the unknown, the invisible, the formless
completeness.
A wonderful feeling of earthiness, heaviness, and
vastness is spreading in your silent "by yourselfness."
Unexpected manifestation: union of Guru-disciple-
and-the-third, the trinity, the harmony of the
principle of three.

Final truths – nothing to change, all to be adjusted to;
A cool reality that dominates in death as in birth.
Guruji also is more still and in meditative questioning.
Somehow one knows all, but still cannot look through.
Ganga Mata's waves whisper and smile and conquer.
"I will care for you. Follow, my foolish children."

Soon everybody gets to know, but does not talk.
You go on the way of nature as before,
Surely nothing has changed.
Your communion with Paramatman[67] remains the goal, the source, and the path.
Your family enjoys the coming event as is normal,
But this being back in the normalcy of worldly life starts clouding over your imagination.
"Maybe you have now to take care about your two bodies."
"No, no, not more, not special."
Your support is the Supreme.
You will not feed on apples and greens, but on the holy scriptures: "Baghavad Puran" and "Shiva Puran" have become your only friends.
You read and read -
Dissolve and escape.
Proud, divine dreams start filling days and sleepless nights:

---

[67] The Universal Soul.

The divine child, your Krishna, Ram, the Savior, the
Incarnation,
Sweet illusion – Mahamaya – moha[68]
That sweeps away all mothers when carrying an
exceptional child.

Guruji, as usual, avoids any privacy and familiarity,
which is thankfully appreciated.
Somewhat more caring in little things:
An unexpected smile, a fruit, a flower, a warm cloth
to spread on the ground to sleep on, this drives
deep-rooted tears out of your being.
You weep: a last feeble attempt to apologize for the
Maya you could not prevent from happening.
Doomed to a happiness of forced parentage,
Unchangeable through a past curse that could turn
into a blessing.
A Guru's presence is always the form of wisdom and
teaching;
Whatever happens to you is the teaching of the
Guru.
This time unfolding the consequences of former life.
"We have unknowingly always lived together,
struggling to lift the lotus from the mud up the stem
to the blossom."
From darkness and ignorance, to light.
When attachment and pleasure are left behind, the
gold is near.

---

[68] Sentimentality

The bright star of Dharma must have been there to bring you to your last marriage, a painful enjoyment in renouncement.
The sufferings of your austerity bring sweet memories.
A thousand pains for your Lord are better than one worldly laugh.
Guruji is with you in heaven or in hell.
One day all will come to one "now."
The island is long left behind.
One time you were sent to the ascetics, your beloved respected Saints, now living your once-lived Ganga-Shiva life.
Your heart will remain under the trees and the stars, alone with the Divine – your Beloved.
"The earth is your bed
The sky your cover
The winds your clothes
The waves and air your food."

If your little ascetic heart of ten years old is weeping to leave the freedom of the ever free,
What about your Guruji, the Son of Shiva, the eternal Yogi?
Even the gods move according to the immortal wheel of change: from the unmanifest to the manifest.
You will also survive in the supreme, following the law of your Master.

Time passes and ripens into the unknown change.
No plans, no preparations

No care, no fear –
Just faith.
Awaiting, awakening.
The Saints are coming, the Gurus of your Guru, the Seers, the Knowers:
Whatever happens fulfills the Divine will.
Only the worldly ones judge and establish a morality to be followed, thinking you must act and thereby prevent events from happening.
The saintly fathers and heavenly friends from long, long past lifetimes support your heavy condition with the smile of understanding,
Even remembering their own lives of before.
We all go on and leave behind one skin after the other to reach the goal of the ever pure.
"Enjoy the suffering and happiness to the utmost in this very life."
Guruji stands firm to His truthfulness:
Nothing to hide or to apologize for.
Not your will is visible, but the Almighty's only and forever.

TWO

Cycles of Maya

Birth
Time comes closer –
Maybe today or tomorrow.
You absolutely don't know.
In the new developing rough ashram Guruji is living
with some disciples and serving devotes who are all
boys and men who keep quiet and overlook your
condition.
Devotees are coming and going, decently leaving
their wives at home.
The village mothers tried to interfere and offer help
but you are too isolated in your divine communion.
Up to now, happy to have God alone as your support
and help.
Having always avoided any contact with women and
deliveries you know really nothing about what will
happen after which signs.
One clear wintry Sunday morning you wake up in a
special mood of celebration and also a strange
painful uneasiness.
"Take a bath with hot water in the ruin quarters."
Guruji says, not really knowing how to involve
Himself into this new precarious situation.
It gets cold and rainy and stormy.

Restlessness and an unbearable pain starts and

drives you out of the ashram, so as not to disturb the vibration.

Guruji's mind follows while sitting in meditation.

Alone by the banyan tree you cannot help screaming to call Mother Earth, the gods, and goddesses.

One old grandmother from the village discovers you and brings some hot ghee[69] and milk.

You drink it, but even now not aware that birth is near – you leave all help and move down to the little river by the ashram's jungle side.

Night falls early and you find shelter in the roots of a tree to scream and scream, giving up protection and care.

An endless and unforgettable time follows: rain, cold, pain, and loneliness.

Then Guruji finds you, He had gone to the former owner of the land to ask his wife how to proceed.

They gave some money. As usual we have nothing, never having saved anything for special occasions.

A taxi is brought to bring you to Rishikul Hospital where some of Guruji's disciples are doctors.

With Guruji's smiling help, you climb up the stony way to the ashram and the street and then begins a ride to the hospital – one scream and rolling on the ground of the taxi.

You cannot think anymore of pleasing God and your Guru, you have become only nature involved in yourself.

---

[69] Purified butter

It is night when we enter the hospital. Guruji is asked to wait outside, surrounded by friendly, joking disciples.

Half an hour later, between consciousness and unconsciousness, the cry of birth is there and then silence.

It's done and you fall into nothingness and emptiness.

"Where are the clothes for the child and yourself?"
Nothing!

Whoever had a thought for clothes: not for the moment and certainly not for the next ones.

"A boy, big and bright!"

You see Guruji's appearance unable to hide a certain joyfulness.

A wakeful sleep follows.

Outside is thunder and lightening and storm and rain.

No longer exposed to nature, for the first time since your birth by the Ganga you are in a room protected and stretched out on a bed and having the unknown warmth of a good blanket.

"Just like Krishna's birth in rain and thunder!"

You dream the mother's dream that her child is the most exceptional in the world.

Guruji, who loves all as His own children, sees Himself bringing tiny clothes from you don't know where, and sweets, and one rose for you.

The nurses quickly encircle Him full of devotion – the

Divine appears in the hospital.
They will certainly get whatever they wish.
To the senior nurse a she-calf is promised.
Guruji is there by the door telling stories from your
sadhu island life.
You lean back, the child in your arms still more than
half of yourself and you smile, having accepted all in
all and whatever will be given in the future.

As the news spread, some financial support flows in
by Ganga Mata's motherly care, but also aversive
forces lift up to destroy the image of a Saint, to drag
down pure devotion into the profane.
Your inner peace and bliss makes you indifferent.
A few more days, you start feeling and appreciating
the comfort that is necessary for the newborn.
For the first time, you will have to take care of
yourself for the sake of the other who is also
yourself.
Seeing your own Self in another being had never
become so strong and identifying.
Living for the one and the second.
Divine life overflows from its innocence and sweet
drinking smiles to flow back into its heavenly origin.
Your meditation becomes a motherly love of
interflowing, still alone with your child in the Infinite.
Soon movement, sounds, and action will start and
slowly but determinedly will pull you out of this
purity, and the fight against distraction will start.

Karma Sannyasa[70]
At least twenty years of worldly engagement are
waiting for you.
Will you be able to hold your karma sannyasa?
You close your eyes and see Guruji sitting in Santosh
beside Shiva the Lord in His heavenly abode.
Your Atman flows around in devotion.
"Narvadaji, I am here."
Guruji's all knowing smile looks in.
"Yes, yes, soon you will become stronger to play the
divine and terrestrial play."
Another day somebody from the ashram comes to
bring you "home."
Your home had always been your soul, where your
Lord resides.
Now the world wants you to have a home for your
child, protection, and comfort to live, to eat, to
study, to die.
Guruji thought to work hard for the new Mahant[71],
To move into the plans of the future.
It will be up to this sweet little one to justify his
birth.

Guruji painted the ruins of the ashram to welcome
him, arranged a room and even a four-legged bed
with a quilt and a pillow!
"Well, now no more escape. Is that where your
austerity was leading to?"
But no use of sarcasm.

---

[70] Renunciation in action.
[71] Heir, caretaker of the Ashram.

You should better help Guruji, your Eternal Yogi, to
live through this new experience of worldly condition,
caused by God's divine Maya but manifested through
your own imperfect existence.
Silent tears cannot help.
You will have to learn to fulfill your motherhood, not
by force, but in devotional obedience.
You will sing your little son of God to sleep with the
mantras.

More and more Saints come to stay and play with the
newborn Ganga Puri, demonstrating how beautiful
the divine Maya is, how pleasant it makes the world,
where God himself plays in childish innocence.
You look on, Guruji looks on.
Holy men with white beards and ashes become
children themselves to meet with the Supreme in the
depth of the world.
God is truth – all is Brahman, the Omniscient.
Ganga Mata smiles: Her Maya game is working well.
Guruji's playful Santosh demonstrates the dream of
illusion.
Was not the first image of Maya Lord Vishnu as a
newborn child floating on a lotus leaf?
A dream to go through.

The day will come to awake and rise again.
Maya cannot avoid duality: happiness and suffering.
On the island these two had been understood as one
and were discarded as unimportant intruders to be
chased away and abandoned.

But now the Divine itself was turned into Maya's reality: you could not just kick it away and throw it into the waves or to the flames to finish with it.
Now you were bound to take care of it, to make it grow, to become strong – to achieve a transformation back to its real nature.
Gently, with Guruji's guidance, your normal life of austerities comes back from a hospital journey where you experienced the infinite law of nature to be born into manifestation.
If illusion would not spread its web, you would not suffer Paradise's loss.

Guruji's unshakable routine of yogic practice: getting up at two o'clock, japa[72], dhyana[73], cow seva, giving all and keeping nothing, had become His divine nature and an encouraging light for the weak disciple to struggle after.
The ten years of training proved to be successful: Soon you saw that you were able to conquer the temptation of a budding householder life with a continuous spirituality flourishing in all activities.
How glad to see that the responsibilities to your child did not prevent you from getting up early for the Aarti puja and doing seva.

Little Ganga Puri soon had to experience that loud unnecessary screaming was not appreciated, especially in the Aarti time and one powerful

---

[72] Repetition of a mantra using a mala/rosary.
[73] Meditation.

"Hum[74]!!" from Guruji would stop further tries to
establish a child's kingdom in the ashram.
The little soul enjoyed the peaceful mantra sounds
by drinking milk and sleeping in mother's lap.
Time shows its power through growth.
Little Ganga Puri's birth and brightness smoothly
overcame beginning rumors and enmities, and
brought peace, prosperity, and happy creativity into
our ashram life.

Guruji transformed the ruin full of snakes and
scorpions and fearful vibrations into a place of
worship and charity.
The barren land flourished with wheat, rice, and
maize, flowers, and vegetables.
"I was born in a cornfield" Guruji once said, "my
body is the land to cultivate and feels the time to
grow or to harvest."
Saints often visited us and fully appreciated the
Divine will manifested in our ashram life.
Besides worldly ups and downs, the mantras, the
scriptures, and the hymns of the Aarti purified little
Ganga Prince's start into his prior heavenly life.
An affection, which Guru and disciple had never
allowed themselves in the bliss of austerity, filled the
unique friendship of mother and child.
It is always the Divine love that you are
experiencing, sometimes from friend to friend, father
to son, mother to child, or between life partners.

---

[74] Seed mantra used by the Goddess to destroy the enemy.

Life had cheered up for you, for Guruji, and the
Saints around, being presented with a beautiful living
toy: Krishna Lila – Krishna Gopal[75].
Nature itself escaped roughness and too much
seriousness by a playful mood.
Purity and divinity make heaven out of any
circumstances.

Maya's Unavoidable Play
For two or three years we lived as a divine family.
Unknown relatives appeared from abroad to care
about their little Ganga Puri, offered some plays, and
then disappeared.
Your sister again prepared, with admirable sacrifices,
a last and final entry into Haridwar, the Gate of
Heaven.
Again she came with your mother, her son, now
grown up into a strong youngster of eighteen, and
other sisters of the soul.
In all her spirituality and renouncement your sister
had a beautiful respect for creation and showed love
and care towards all its miraculous forms and plays.
Seeing the child born out of Ganga waves,
meditation, and service to cows, and Guru and Divine
Mother tumbling towards them wearing wooden
sandals, a long shirt, and beaming in divine
remembrance, your remaining family members were
more than touched with bliss.
Not that the child belonged to us, but better, we had

---

[75] God Krishna's life drama; Gopal is one of Krishna's names as a
child

become a part of his innocent world.

There was love all around, devotion, respect, and service.

Your mother enlarged and stabilized the financial condition.

All in all, Guruji became more friendly-minded in front of your kind mother, and His divine anger disappeared for longer periods of time.

Buffaloes were bought and more land for wheat and grass was cultivated.

Maya was pushing forward its unavoidable play.

Your mother's and sister's renouncement and spirituality increased, enjoying simplicity and bliss through the mantra.

Your mother got initiation and a rudraksh mala, and a long white raw silk shirt as her only possessions.

Her mind became peaceful and was shining with compassion and friendliness to all.

"Ram, Ram, OM, Hari OM, OM Namah Shivaya, OM Namo Narayan", was her only vocabulary with which she managed to share company with the people around.

At four o'clock in the morning she joined the coldwater bath, the Aarti puja by the fire, and the meditation.

With her grandson, the morning was spent walking around the cows and buffaloes in the jungle by the Ganga riverside.

All her worries and problems disappeared, setting a beautiful example that by giving all to the Guru, the representation of Dharma, your mind settles in peace and enjoys joy and positiveness.

It had been she who, since childhood, had reminded us to sacrifice our concentration to the divine, the eternal good, the scriptures, the art of music and poetry,

And to renounce sensual attachments and involvement in worldly pleasures, and to be aware of the limitations of married life.

She allowed us to spend days in nature and retreat instead of going to school and supported your long trips to lonely places by the seaside to find Truth in isolation.

Now she saw, in our renounced way of living, the fulfillment of her own dreams.

Only for her children had she agreed to a marriage, maybe to achieve through us what she had been unable to.

Full of enthusiasm she jumped into the lake of the eternal song of Ram Ram and OM Namah Shivaya. Sometimes a voice from her inside complained that she was not really able to understand the mantra, its purification, and its light.

"To learn the Vedic culture, the nature of Ram, from the very beginning through childhood would still make a difference."

Wishes appearing in the end of one's life certainly manifest into a next life.

So it came that two girls were born: Guruji always

liked to exhaust all in one life.

Three years after Ganga Puri's birth, Mandakini[76] was born.

Mandakini started her journey into this life strong and determined to serve Guruji and her father's Maya. Brought up, taken care of, and utterly enjoyed by your sister and your mother.

Once Maya spreads its web, time loses itself and seems to run from one enchanting illusion to the next.

You learned more and more to accept and trust in the divine will just by listening to the song of the soul seeking to liberate itself from bondage and to protect and warn you of further involvement.

Nature wants to expand all over and dissolve everything into its mystery.

A sad passivity bound you to the law of creation – there had always been the dream to change life according to your own individuality. "Was it possible? "Could it be?" "How to?"

Your gift of humility and service to Guruji created a waiting phase for both of us: to exhaust forever a life-long attachment.

This should be the final round of a worldly relation, no more an engagement but to observe your obligatory duty imposed by the law of cause and effect.

Attachments drop, not by avoiding them, but only by

---

[76] The heavenly Ganga River at Kedarnath, the abode of Lord Shiva.

living them out in devotion and faith.

Death and Birth Again
The last child of Maya's power will be born shortly
after your Mother's spectacular death, as foretold by
Guruji, to complete the fulfilling rounds of her life.
How could there be a new life when you had since
long abandoned the pleasure for its support?
You become weak and exhausted but life energy
doesn't finish.
The more Maya you give out and destroy, the more it
spreads.
Your mother, when she faced the coming birth, at
once lost life courage, became reserved as if
knowing that it was time to give up, to prepare for a
fresh endeavor. "We are not going to Gangotri[77]?"
she shyly asked. "No, this time it doesn't look like
it."
At the end of the season, Gangotri[78] will be born to
carry out a soul's attempt to achieve liberation.
On the first day of the nine days of Navratri[79] your
mother seemed to be called to join the Universal
Mother.
After the usual morning puja she took leave from
Guruji, the cows, and her daughters to retreat for the
following nine days into a complete fast and a silent
kind of Samadhi.
No suffering, no complaints, no wish.

---

[77] Source of the Ganga River.
[78] The third child, Alaknanda, is nick-named Gangotri.
[79] Nine days of fasting in spring and fall for Durga Mata, the
Mother of the Universe.

Sometimes she woke up from her divine dream,
opened her eyes shining a heavenly bliss, recognizing
us without attachment.
Her world seemed to be in no comparison with our
limited and bounded one.
She even embraced Guruji, pointing out the precious
value of the mala He had given her.
A few moments were there to share with us, only to
fall back into another mindless dream.
Your sister sacrificed her Navratri fast to meditate
day and night by her side:
A last puja for the oneness of your worldly and
heavenly mother.

You had been too much interwoven into Mother
Nature's web: your puja had to be all practical,
experiencing the invisible change of the dying soul
and its transformation into the coming individual
soul.
Your body suffered and with it the mind and the
intellect.
Your soul, the ever-young, escaped to the land of
neither birth nor death, nor pain nor happiness, to
rest and enjoy the bliss of the Self-Illumined light.
Life's heaviness called you back; you are not living
for yourself my dear soul!

On the ninth day, when the Goddess' bells are
ringing throughout India,
When the Mother is worshiped all over in the form of
little virgins,

When heaven is open for the Motherly abode,
Your mother opened and closed her eyes for the last
time, to join her daughter's song of
Om Namah Shivaya,
Throwing herself into the Light of the other world.
While one daughter was praying by her side, the
other, already carrying her next birth, was offering
flowers to Ganga Mata's waves.

When you wandered back with fruits and flowers,
your ashram had changed into the veil of dissolution.
People and Saints had gathered in front and, from
somewhere inside, Guruji's unimaginable emotional
scream
"Narvadaji!"
Reached your heart to break the last cut of human
relation:
Your mother had left her mortal shell to fly into the
Infinite where beginning and end are meeting.
The first meeting with death in your life at the time
when all your being prepared for birth.

You bowed down to the law of dissolution.
Since your childhood you had always adored the end
of this mortal bondage.
Death had become known as the unknown friend to
take you to the other shore.
The Saints around celebrated the auspicious day of
her departure, the victory of the immortal soul over
the temporary body.
Little Ganga Puri looked with wide-open eyes from

the corner: normal life for the first time had been
interrupted by something unexpected that had to be
understood.
Mandakini didn't like to hold any more the loving
hand she used to play with.

The palanquin was decorated with fruits, balloons,
and flowers.
In her last white dress your mother was seated – you
remember her white smile and her hands like playing
her last piano concert.
On the shoulders of the Saints she was carried to
Ganga Mata's Samadhi stall[80] to be drowned into the
holy waters.
Her golden rings and teeth, a Bhagavad Gita, the
rudraksh mala went with her former life.
A beautiful celebration full of light and colors,
balloons and flowers.

The highest sacrifice one can bring, to allow one's
own life energy to fly back to the home of one's soul.
How long our desires and ego consciousness have
tied the body into attachment of illusionary ideas.
To the knower of the soul, death loses its blackness
and fear.
What a joy when finally the cage opens and you can
freely fly to where you came from.
Your mother had left the normal emptiness, a reality
that doesn't need words or attributes.

---

[80] Place for water Samadhi – drowning place for Sannyasins.
(Worldly people go to burning ghats.)

Often on the roof we heard a joyful call from the
mango tree, my sister even saw her white hands
playing the piano in the Ganga water:
Her last water symphony.
A big charitable celebration was held, many Saints
were invited and given donations. Even now her
friendliness and cheerfulness is remembered.

One month later the last child's birth floated as the
third river Alaknanda[81] into our ashram, after
Mandakini and Ganga.
The holy names served the divine creation: God in
child's form.
Faithfully, all was appreciated but nature's heaviness
and gross form weighed hard on you,
As balls on the bird's wing,
Was Maya going to tie you down?
The immense loss of prana caused an emptiness that
even the sweet innocence of the newborn could
hardly fill.
When Saints, your heavenly family from long, long
lives ago, came for congratulations, you couldn't help
weeping, demonstrating such an entanglement in
your yogic life.
You sank back and surrendered to the little newborn
life energy, born to live life in all its brightness and
shadows.
You always had been obliged to the light of hope in
your children's eyes.

---

[81] Heavenly Ganga River (tributary) at Badrinath, the abode of
Lord Vishnu.

Such an innocent demand and right for a beautiful
peaceful life to enjoy and to be shared.
If you give life, it is for preservation not for
destruction.
You might have to join the illusionary game, thereby
gently clinging to the Truth beyond.

THREE

The Divine Family

For you, the unavoidable family life is transformed into a divine family by the abandonment of all attachment, desire, and emotions.

Through motherhood your devotional path is able to advance through constant and total sacrifice and unselfishness, without which God cannot be approached nor realized.

Time in this illusion passes in a remarkable speediness, whereas time in meditation is eternal and keeps its fixed impression in the mind.

Six years of three childbirths and their play – sometimes you don't know what difference has actually come into your life.

The relation to your own soul and to the souls around you always remains the same.

There is you and your Guruji and the deep devotion for Shiva, the Eternal, the Separated One from all beings.

From this constant ecstasy the eyes and heart are shining and transmitting their brightness to all the world outside, with all its troubles and seeming disharmony.

Guruji and you, His eternal disciple child, had always been happy like this, remaining the same in the same place, while events were circling around,

And the form of Maya, coming and going, one time in front and then one time in back, sometimes pleasant and sometimes not.

The dream goes on, one followed by the next.

One day this illusion will be exhausted and you will sit in reality as before.

You have seen Guruji from time eternal by the side of Lord Shiva – a humble shadow, the eyes down, as the Lord Himself.

Being sent into this mortal world, sacrificing all, only to hold one's enjoyment of the Eternal.

Why should a little playfulness with His own children not be allowed?

Enjoyment belongs to the world and its Maya, and is therefore rejected and discarded by the realized soul.

Guruji liked to tell the story of the Neem Rishi:

For thousands of years, the Rishi licked at the Neem Tree[82] to satisfy his hunger.

A heavenly nymph sent by God Indra smeared honey on the Neem Tree.

Slowly the traps of sweet taste awakened his body consciousness. He opened his eyes to fall into the attraction of the senses.

He married the nymph and they had many children for a long time.

One day he experienced himself surrounded by all his children, one on his head, one on his shoulder, one pulling his beard, one twisting his arm, … what

---

[82] Tree known for its bitter taste and healing qualities.

happened? The Rishi stood up, freed himself from the children, and went back to the Neem Tree.

Having taken the form of the many you have to dive and dissolve deep:
Soon you will find the gap to escape.
This gap, always present, has to be taken by our renouncement – hopping onto the endless between the moving limitations.
You know the time will come when the Real of your life, the No-More-Ending will shine over your illusions, which will fall like the moths that fall as soon as they touch the light.

The children had to grow into the many made up rules and forms, and do their best to integrate into a life of illusionary forms. The habits anchor into a reality to overpower the subtle truths of the soul.
Guruji and yourself paid in the coin of responsibility for giving birth to world citizens, giving in to ties and belts, to run to be in time, at the risk of forgetting the bliss of eternity.
Time has to be filled up with books and bags and the marks for wrong and right.

A mother's highest recommendation is when her child chooses the spiritual path of wisdom.
The future will tell, God's grace will show its degree as fruit of your service.
Throughout the years of our divine family life, the children growing up into their destined beings,

Guruji had always been in peaceful indifference,
caring with love and affection or with fear and
respect, causing strictness, while lacking all feelings
of sentimentality or privacy.
Guruji always remained the fakir demonstrating that
while resting in Divine Consciousness one was able
to serve the Supreme will in any form;
Having cows, preparing and distributing food for all,
or living the family life with all its good and bad –
Everything on the base of the two to four o'clock
morning meditations.
You followed, never missing the morning bath and
puja, sometimes with a child sleeping under your
shawl while sitting in the lotus position.

The continuous readings of the "Shiva Puran" and
"Bhagavad Puran" transformed every day life into a
divine Maya.
Beautiful like all children, the three grew up in all
their innocence,
Maybe more disciplined and showing more
seriousness and joy deriving from an inside source.
A most preferable environment of Saints, cows, the
holy Ganga, the devotional vibration of the mantras
throughout, the scriptures, a charitable life rhythm,
For example never to eat before the cows had gotten
their food and at least five to ten souls had been
given food.

As all great souls, Guruji's individual soul was the
soul of all,

His happiness spread onto all around Him,
Others' suffering or trouble was His own suffering.
Laziness, doubt, unawareness, and carelessness,
were enemies who had to be chased away,
Not with explanatory words but with punishment
exploding in divine anger.

On the island we had lived on what Ganga Mata was
giving, even then His soul was demanding more for
the welfare of the cows or the people staying around
Him.
His suffering soul became angry, thereby forcing Ma
Ganga to fulfill His charitable wishes to avoid harm
and destruction through Guruji's anger.
Now having a registered land, the responsibility
increased.
The most awful thing to imagine for Guruji was to be
unable to serve His guests.
Possessing a valuable ashram and not being able to
give freely was a nightmare for Him.
"What is the use of piling up bricks if you are not
able to give sufficiently to all?" He would say.
This principle of charity had been Guruji's seed of
austerity.
Through this we escaped the pangs of Maya,
continuing a life in self-sacrifice, devotion and
service.

With Guruji's fakir nature there was no chance to fall
into the settlement of a householder life.
As usual, whatever came in was spent the same day,

so that the fees, the electricity bill, each pencil, were
based on austerity followed by Guruji's angry
outburst, making yourself responsible for the inflow
of Maya into His ever free and independent sadhu
life.
How much your heart was with him, how much you
wanted to lose yourself in meditation
Or run to the end of the beginning –
But the escape was forbearance in silent love,
devotion, and faith.
The long service to the cows seemed to have blessed
you with their nature: "Narvadaji is like a cow[83]"
was one of the few compliments Guruji blessed you
with.

Time passed while internally thanking Ganga Mata
for the blessing of right understanding of God's
mysterious ways.
You don't know how you would have survived if
temptations of wealth and comfort would have
swallowed Guruji's truthfulness and spirituality.
One determination: to sacrifice your life to Guruji's or
God's service, in whatever form the divine was
represented to you.

Still – an indigestible shadow is lying like a stone
inside your being, holding you to the normal,
preventing you from loving God in His most simple
form, without any "what fors" or "whys."

---

[83] Symbol of humility and forbearance.

Still to learn that the divine will in the form of former karmas has to be exhausted, and not according to your dream call for liberation:
You remember some mistakes in your previous karma that forced you to suffer the householder life Instead of being blessed with a sole concern of spirituality.
What is a greater sacrifice for one who has once renounced, than to perform duties as a householder?
In the midst of the enlightened ones, you are carrying a boulder or a cross that in reality does not exist.
"Why not take everything as equally pleasant?" the wise would smile.
Surely, but the "still" would not disappear.
Born with tears in your eyes, you will go on carrying loads, injuries, incapacities, enjoyments, and momentary distractions.
Hiding the pain inside but at the same time awakening to the pure light announcing itself from behind the mountain.
In between all action there is always an eternity to melt your worldliness into the cry and flow of devotion.

And so you suffer – more an upside down suffering of not being willing to accept the most normal and worldly.
Still you cling inseparably to the divine and steal its golden glow to paint your world secretly for the coming day that cannot be not lived.

It is the illusion of a coming liberation that hinders you
From accepting the now as a beautiful gift.
You smile into the dark Indian eyes of your three children
And join again Guruji's lotus position and His meditation of Santosh.
Invisible helpers go on supporting the growth of Ganga Mata's "Maya children."

Since early childhood you had prayed for death, for the "all is over – finished," not sad or depressed, more looking forward to when your time on earth would run out.
Now death was more than the end of the suffering:
Death had become the promised gate to liberation into wisdom and light – the end of the pilgrimage, the reward for your sacrifices.
Maya had tied you through the inner sense of your heavenly children:
"You stay here and fulfill obediently what you have missed in former lives."
Oh yes, you were always thankful for being able to accept God's compassionate thorns and flowers.
Time will pass and time itself is the divine will.
And it passed in the beautiful duality of worldly life:
plays and laughter, smiles and jokes by day, and aloofness for the night meditation.
God is great, Guruji is all, blessing you with more than you could have ever asked for: the rare fruit of wisdom and pleasure, divine ecstasy and its dry

practice.

After the passing away of your mother, your sister also tried to separate from Babaji's care and protection.
She began to do austerities on her own, without Guruji's motherly care, a hard and dangerous way for a new initiate.
Perhaps driven by the quest to experience more divinity on earth than that which her karma would provide her.
She left the ashram on the full moon dedicated to the Guru, leaving all that Babaji, with admirable responsibility, had settled to secure her ascetic life in India along the Ganga,
In order to search for a deeper realization or to enjoy the so-called freedom of the sadhu life.
After some excursions she came back, mostly out of responsibility to look after the growing children.
She always thought that her younger sister was too old inside to show the beaming happiness and playfulness that a young mother should have.

Your sister stayed some more years by making pilgrimages to Badrinath and making offerings of tulsi malas[84] to the Lord.
Before the Kumbha Mela of Allahabad, twelve years after her initiation there, she left for her native land to live with her son to build an ashram and serve the

---

[84] Made from the seeds of the Holy Basil plant.

Western mind with Eastern spirituality.

Nine years of comings and goings of your family
members in the ashram,
And then again the initial state of Ganga, Guru and
yourself.
Still searching and sometimes having found the
Supreme Lord inside and outside.
Living life in Guruji's training had created a wonderful
harmony and equal-mindedness for all events and
the different people passing through the ashram.
All devotees and seekers of truth had become your
brothers and sisters of the soul.
Many came sent by the divine Himalayan breeze
supporting our living on faith and truth.
Interestingly many became inspired by your divine
family life as an austerity, in seclusion and in the
world equally.
In between physical activities, the fire worship, and
the consoling words of Lord Krishna in "The
Bhagavad Gita," the mantras, the yoga postures, the
pranayamas[85] all shone forth.
Sometimes a little group came together on the roof
for a dissolution in the sunset meditation.

How to fly behind the clouds or in the deep space of
your soul when Guruji's physical presence was
around, maybe in need of something or other.
You would run down and find fulfillment just by

---

[85] Practices working with breath and prana, life force.

staying near Him.

The grace of seva was given to you for the time being, bearing higher flowers than did attempted night meditations and fasts.

When Guruji occasionally had been rightly angry, then you were given the capacity to stand on one leg for the rest of the night or embrace the Shiva lingam as your last protection and relief.

Guruji's divine anger diminished to rare seasonal outbursts of nature, like thunder and lightening, to fertilize the earth.

Like a storm without clouds – Guruji's "Shiva the Destroyer" nature revolted and shook all the three worlds of our ashram.

Its inhabitants, thrown into hidden corners, experienced that outer pleasure and comfort are only temporary, reminding them never to forget the immortal inside.

As furious and terrible as it was, still there was teaching.

Guruji locked Himself up for three days without food or water, unbearable for you because all service was denied: Guruji's grace, your life prana, was cut.

How confident one is in happiness and comfort!

Only the hopelessness of hell shows the light of bliss.

The austerity went on in the disguise of a family life.

Guruji's soul of a renunciate had a natural allergy to worldly comfort and facilities, privacies and sentimentalities.

Maya's flower mostly was sacrificed before its petals opened to pour out the forthcoming seeds.

How thankful you were, how your heart and mind admired His yogic greatness to hold the ascetic fire burning.

The phenomenal is doomed to pass, whereas the formless silence awaits to embrace you again in its virgin innocence.

Guruji made you understand the eternal wheel of change and time;

You smiled, in all involvements, the smile of the eternal truth.

Formal Ties

Our eternal light marriage from lives and lives had to be solemnized; the births of the divine soul into the form had to be certificated.

Guruji - pressing His teeth together - would not show His long matted beard to the office servants to explain the divine play of Mother Ganga.

Devotees came in to help and brought the whole marriage magistrate with advocate, stamps, and signs, to our ashram, and a court[86] ceremony was created with flowers, witnesses, and an encircling[87] of the only table in the ashram. The marriage magistrate, turning himself into a lifelong devotee, took Guruji's holy hand to fix His thumbprint on the paper.

---

[86] A court ceremony can legalize a Hindu marriage, (provide a certificate).

[87] Seven circles are made for a marriage bond to be formed.

How Guruji's heart must have tightened to feel the
consequences of fulfilling the heavenly curse on us.
For Him the ever-free, proud son of God who never
allowed anybody to make Him write or read for the
world's illusionary servantship.

Certificates were made but all possible happiness or
contentment was missing. We both stayed quiet,
avoiding all discourses: life forces one into
compromises, the tax for its so-called enjoyment.

You couldn't help or contribute to this process, now
unfortunately more tight-lipped: you had run away
from these conventions to storm into a paradise of
sacrifice and austerities.

The Wheel of Time Survives

Om Nama Shivaya – Jai Ganga, Omkare – Jai Sita
Ram.

These were the keys to open the treasure of the
world of Dharma.

You couldn't just educate the children into what you
had left so long ago.

Were you induced to leave the playground of Lord
Krishna?

Was the world to make you descend from the
heavenly abodes, while withstanding boldly all the
temptations of Maya?

Not all lost – the worldly game was played in your
Seven Rishis ashram in Anand Van, the Valley of
Bliss, where the holy OM of the Vedas is still sung,
where the Ganga Goddess is dancing down from
Shiva's hair locks to pass the mortal world to dissolve

into the ocean of the netherworlds.

Is She not also gracefully fulfilling Her curse to live
on earth as a blessing to mankind? Soon Her time
will be over; the world will weep and remember Her
legends but She will rejoice to go back to Her
heavenly abode.

On earth the illusion of time weighs heavy, causing
hopelessness and suffering, you can only live a
memory of your Real Light heritage.

Have courage: the Divine Soul comes with you to go
through all these hardships knowing the way to lead
you back.

OM – Shri Guru Deva.

The blessing had always been with the unavoidable.
Time passed well and quickly.

A good western education for the children could be
afforded from the nakedness of their father's
asceticism.

Never having anything but always all necessities
were given through the invisible magic of the divine
heritage.

Sometimes Guruji took on the challenge: that He, the
poor fakir having nothing, being nothing, knowing
nothing, could feed from His nothingness hundreds
of people, hold ten to twenty cows and land together
with the workers, and even a high level education for
His children – just by never asking for anything other
than for "life after life in renunciation."

A best possible English medium school was found for

all of them. The boy was even sent to a boarding
school to concentrate on worldly studies, to stay
away from the holy fire and the ashram life.
Once when there was no option for the fees, a letter
arrived and a long forgotten friend of your childhood
offered his financial support for the next five years.

When once you had come to look into the classroom
of the primary school you saw little Ganga Puri
standing on the desk and proclaiming Sanskrit
prayers with all his schoolmates looking on.
Tears blinded your eyes and you carried your
austerity child home like a precious first prize trophy.

The girls, in all their exceptional sweetness from
being brought up among cows, Saints, and mantras,
tried their best to enjoy a normal children's life, to be
or become like the others, with mama-papa-kids.
The time also came when they suffered silently,
listening for any possible offence for being children
of a renunciate.

Guruji's power was Santosh and an open revolt or
disagreement had never been allowed.
Through the example of their mother who had
experienced the power of endurance, the hardest
storms could pass while keeping the eyes down.
The heart would weep, not out of anger or suffering,
but in a loving devotion to bear all possible hardships
for the divine purification.
The boy got his separate room to study, to dream, to

weep by himself during times of lonely problem
solving.

His Babaji and Mataji would not and could not come
to sit on his bed and hold his hand.

Their love and blessings reached only through night-
long meditations and not by showing affection.

Faith in the Heavenly Father and Mother had to
conquer sentimentalities.

Worldly consolation won't prove successful, not in
childhood, and certainly not when grown up.

At the age of three, a Pandit awakened in Ganga Puri
the verses of the "Bhagavad Gita," the "Ramayan,"
and ancient Sanskrit mantras. The fifteenth, twelfth,
and fifth chapters of the "Bhagavad Gita" were
recited by heart like a celestial parrot – a bliss that
lightened away all the sacrifices and compromises of
a worldly life.

Karma from former lives had them be born into this
renunciate environment both as a blessing and as a
chance to hold the last step on the worldly ladder to
dive forever into the formless ocean of bliss, or being
throw out of heaven to experience once more worldly
limitations and temptations to choose once more and
clearly: a position on earth or renouncement in
liberation from bondage.

A mother's highest recommendation is when her
child chooses the spiritual path of wisdom.

You silently prayed to God and the Ganga that they
might prove to be children of ascetics, not born of
sensual pleasure but out of solemn love and devotion

to God.

Guruji wanted to push them into the world of doctors and officers, official careers: if they are born renunciates, then nothing can stop them from taking the path.

Babaji always tried to retain the treasures for which the Saints renounced the world, to allow the choice between the invisible real and the openly manifested. Guruji and Ganga Mata let the children choose any of the many options, waiting for the right time to pour nectar, and so realize their true Nature.

Ganga Puri wanted to become a pilot in the Airforce, studying mathematics and physics for graduation. Mandakini longed for control and management organization. Alaknanda, to fulfill Babaji's wish to see her as a doctor, chose ayurveda to find her aim in life.

The future will tell, God's grace will show its degree as fruit of your service.

FIVE

The Change Begins

Our ashram life continued based on morning and evening puja, Saints, and cow and Guru service, full of happiness but always restrained through a fear and respect for the higher force above.
Sadhus and devotees passed through the ashram which helped Guruji to maintain an impersonal atmosphere.
A little bit of everything: farming, puja, yoga, lecture, charitable food supply, and care for the old and orphans.

Full moon and new moon celebrations and all the many festivals held the spiritual vibration high.
Two Mahakumbha Melas vibrated powerfully through the ashram, for Babaji and yourself, although not so much for the children who were used to many devotees, Saints, and foreigners and felt normal in their company.
It was a high time, when your heavenly family wandered on earth and one felt Shiva, Parvati, Narvada, Hanuman, the Rishis all around, visible and invisible.

Guruji had always obliged Himself to serve more abundantly to strangers than to His own children.
He could burst out of harmony when the Ganga Mata

could not provide as much as He wanted to give. Anxiously you saw Him suffering and stressing Himself with obligations.

Seeing His storerooms empty, He was giving up His famous Santosh to be happy with what was provided. He, not waiting for Ganga Mata's service, would rush to some devotees to get donations of wheat and rice in the name of Sadhu, Saints, and service.

Most of the time the supernatural power would come over Him to fulfill His determination to serve.

But in the Kumbha Mela of 1986, age and health show their first defeat: Guruji fell down in a brain stroke and recovered outwardly but half-paralyzed. Guruji forced His yogic energy into one lotus position, no talking, no movement.

Throughout the Kumbha Mela Guruji held His satsang[88] by the duni fire, surrounded by devotees, as a silent constant worship and call on Lord Shiva. "Alak Niranjan" (Hail to God, the Separate One)

Only you knew that late at night when all are gone, your powerful Yogi Guru was unable to walk even five or ten meters or talk clearly or move His hands to eat.

A miserable condition in worldly circumstances, but you saw only His Yogic determination to defeat the death of the body and hold the shine of the immortal soul.

---

[88] Company of Truth; chanting, hearing scriptures, or sitting in the company of a Saint.

Like this, as so often in your life, disease and
suffering lose their terminal stage because of the
overpowering strength of faith and devotion.
Months of physical hardships pass in the light of
intense prayer and meditation.

Soon improvement is brought with medical help,
massages, and pure cow ghee.
Guruji manages Himself back toward His former
condition, still the stroke can never be denied, some
of His proud strength is broken.
You fall with Him, attaching yourself to devotional
service to His bodily weakness and need of loving
care.
With every breath you engage yourself to create any
and every facility for His bodily welfare.
In a fever of surrendering you steal every activity
from Guruji's side:
No walk where you do not follow to watch over each
movement, restraining yourself from holding Guruji's
hand or carrying His holy form on your shoulder.
Watching over Guruji's minimized eating, preparing
each drop of water and morsel of food by yourself, in
winter heating the water to bathe
And warming Guruji's clothes to wear with the breath
of your mouth.
No rest without offering massage to Guruji's holy
feet.
Your whole meditation slips into a surrendering
service up to death, over-exaggerating Guruji's
physical care, identifying more with bodily weakness

than with the immortal strength of the soul.

From time to time, Guruji and disciple experience in meditation their two souls united for many lifetimes, and bound again in the attachment to serve each other.

The one part, the higher Self of Guruji, through the loving care of Maya, while being served, is growing deep into an unavoidable manifestation. The other, only a part, a sport, a dream fantasy of the pure soul, is blessed to serve and surrender in the form of illusion, floating united through clouds of time to circle into dissolution:

One day, one breath, one final retention.

To meet and live for love and pray for its ending: the dream has always been a part of the play, to dissolve together back to where we were coming from.

Time has its own rhythm:

You have to move and laugh and weep until all debts are paid.

Like this Guruji's immortality grows older and you do your best to hurry up to become older than old.

One childhood younger than your Guruji, you never tried to avoid any hardships, more living life up than enjoying its charms.

You always worked hard to pull the rotten teeth out, mentally and physically.

Serving Guruji's feet is like humbling yourself into the earth, burying your individuality deep, losing your identity through serving.

Your back bends round to touch constantly God's (Guruji's) feet.

Sweep and clean wherever His feet might move.

You even don't want to straighten up as the next moment you feel you will bow down again.

In your childhood, your little heart had longed for the time to die, to age, to become disabled for the world, now your physical frame plays "old age" whereas your inner being is strong and bright to journey through dissolution of body and mind into eternal youth.

"Stretch up hold yourself straight."

"How old are you? – eighty-five?"

Everybody, your children, all want to hold you strongly anchored into the worldly play.

Even Guruji, who never seemed to acknowledge any change or specialness in your outer appearance, tries to encourage you to fulfill the pilgrimage, as hard it might appear.

Guruji, Himself ever straight without support, sits in the lotus position, bold and in grace, holding the divine will down on earth as a reality.

Yogis realize the strength of the divine soul, thereby conquering all physical limitations, disease, and old age.

The seeker still dies with the body in a self-imposed renunciation.

The bliss of the Self, shining through all illusion, appears as an aim, the goal at the end of austerity.

Even if you wanted, you couldn't allow yourself to

die: before, because of your sweet mother, and now, because of your innocent children and the lifelong service to your Guru.

To die serving God, the Guru's form, appears to you more than heaven.

Certainly you would not be rewarded so easily: just allowed to drop physical limitation, like the pumpkin falling from its stem.

Gently, in all hardships the new light of the other life has to be understood and searched for - the blossom of the lotus piercing the mud,

Leaving behind darkness and ignorance.

A mystical dawn of an unknown awakening.

Buried deep, still in the unconscious, cosmic life energy will lead you to the horizon as it guided you formerly through the wilderness.

How it will be: you looked at Guruji's more or less suffering frame.

Everything He seems to have sacrificed for you: His immortal yogic beauty, His ever-free pride and independence with the Ganga, the Himalayas, the wind, the fire, and the cows, as wish-fulfilling servants.

Out of love for His child's liberation, Guruji will play death to sow the seed of immortality for all the disciples of His game: Guru-Lila.

Still attached to Guruji's Maya you don't dare to think ahead.

Will Guruji let you fall into the support of His higher

being by withdrawing the hand of protection?
Dissolving into your individual spirit to make you live
the strength from inside?
Something happens which makes you beautifully
calm and empty.
Long before dawn, the signs of light announce the
arrival of a new reality.
To understand the law of nature is comforting, like
the caressing hand of your mother swaying you into
the smiling acceptance of the eternal design.
OM Guruji.
Hold me tight in Your yogic vision and open Your
child's ignorant eyes for ever-lasting perception.

OM Shanti OM.

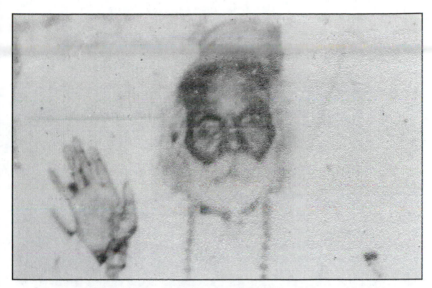

Sthanpati Bhairav Puri, Alakhiya, of Bhairav Akhara, Haridwar.
Guru of Sri Santosh Puri

Babaji and Narvada Puri on the Island, with the cows

The original "Dharmsala" soon after Babaji and Narvada arrived :
the beginnings of Santosh Puri Ashram

Narvada Puri with one of the cows in the Ashram courtyard

Sri Santosh Puri
Baba Avadhut

Babaji and visiting Sadhus at the duni

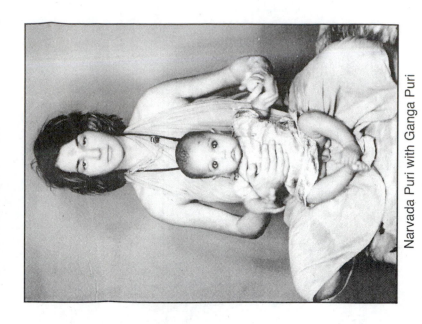

Narvada Puri with Ganga Puri

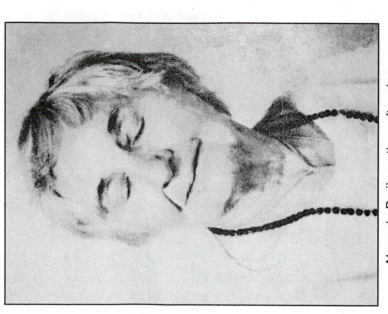

Narvada Puri's mother, after she
settled at Santosh Puri Ashram

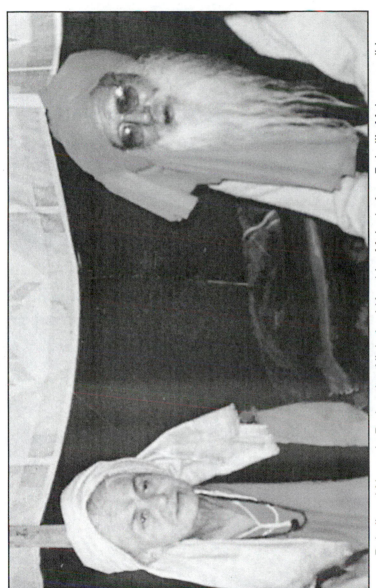

Babaji and Narvada Puri at the Allahabad Kumbha Mela, before Babaji's Mahasamadhi

Babaji's body after Mahasamadhi,
remaining in the lotus posture for entombment

Babaji's Samadhi Temple.
The statue of Babaji and the lingam are over where He is buried

Samadhi Temple in
Ashram garden

Shiva lingam brought from Omkareshwara

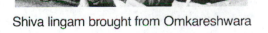

The new "Mahant," Ganga Puri, with Sadhus
from the Juna Akhara

The duni as it looks today

जूनादीठाधीश्वर आचार्य महामण्डलेश्वर
श्री १००८ स्वामी अवधेशानन्द गिरि जी महाराज

Swami Avdheshanand Giri Acharya Mahamandaleshwar
– head of Sri Panch Dasnam Juna Akhara –
who gave the initiation at Ujjain Kumbha Mela

Narvada Puri with Sadhvis (female Sadhus) at the "Royal Bath"
at Ujjain Kumbha Mela

Narvada Puri teaching the Bhagavad Gita

From left to right: Ganga, Mandakini, Narvada, and Alaknanda Puri

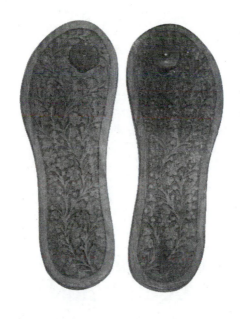

Part Three: Dissolution

Love love love
Love to love
To be
In love
To you
In me
And me
In you.

ONE

Between Life and It's Completion

Time will speak and there is silence –
Frozen silence like facing death.
Remembering when the Divine Song, the Bhagavad
Gita, was spoken by Lord Krishna to Arjuna, when all
the world's illusionary game ends into one eternal
moment: to listen to the Lord's words of Truth, the
seed for liberation.

Guruji announces to go to the Kumbha Mela with a
determination that changes normal activity into
destiny.
Guruji will leave His mortal frame

As His Guru left on the silent new moon, twelve
years ago at the age of 108 years, at the Kumbha
Mela at Allahabad – Prayag[89].
There the confluence of three rivers (Ganga,
Yamuna, Saraswati), corresponding to Samadhi when
the ida nadi (Ganga) and pingala nadi (Yamuna) and
sushumna (Saraswati), join into union at ajna chakra
(Prayag).[90]
Normal words, sent into the morning breeze:
"I will definitely go to the Kumbha Mela."
"Mantra mulam, Guru vakyam:"
My mantra is the word of my Guru.
The Guru's words grasp your heart like claws of
death and hold you raw between earth and heaven.
Where do you want to go?
Down into the weeping emotions and attachments of
the senses or tear off the total of the last suffering
that sticks to your soul and hinders it from flying?
Your wings will grow when you unite in Guruji's
mortal sacrifice, abandoning your only love on earth:
Guruji, your life and prana,
Your death and liberation.

Preparations are made for the beautiful and the
unavoidable.
"Narvadaji will come with me!"

---

[89] Ancient name of Allahabad meaning "confluence of rivers."
[90] The three main nadis (energy channels of the body) are ida
(left channel), pingala (right channel), and sushumna (central
channel), all beginning at the tailbone and merging at the
forehead center (ajna chakra).

Sure, you will go to Allahabad, into the ajna chakra
where all individualities meet in the origin, the ocean
of bliss.
The vacuum stays in your heart, while witnessing
Guruji's Maya, the playing ground of our ashram.
The children are now grown up into charming flowers
in the heavenly garden: Ganga Puri twenty-three,
Mandakini twenty, Alaknanda seventeen.
What will you do? Pray for Guruji's Samadhi?
How could you? You dare not even accept the
thought of an eventual separation.
But do you have the courage to ask the holy Ganga
or the Lord of Life, to continue Guruji's mortal
journey for another Kumbha Mela twelve years
ahead?
Is there any hope in delay?
You fall deep into a new loneliness:
Guruji all around or present,
Will you be able to hold onto the departing soul?
Another reality appears: "We will live and die
together." Guruji often smiled down to you.
The most beautiful agreement of the Guru-disciple
dream.
All will work out according to the divine plan.

Acceptance spreads over Guruji's usually more
disagreeing appearance.
Invitations are usually refused as unnecessary
expenses.
Our ashram was designed to hold Santosh, self-
sufficiency, as its stronghold:

Nothing from outside should be wished for, all happiness and fulfillment to be found in the presence, the silent spot around which all is moving: people, pilgrimages, goods and bads, ups and downs.

This time Guruji smoothly agrees to visit the abode of the gods:

Badrinath.

Guruji enjoying the divine Himalayan beauty in calm detachment.

All of a sudden He becomes immune against physical hardships and the normal indigestion.

Guruji, the eternal form of Brahman the Supreme, Never sick nor weak nor aging.

Was it you who had lost and weakened yourself in identifying His immortality with the physical frame and the dependency on worldly circumstances?

Still, could you harden your emotions and serve less or care half-heartedly for Guruji's ailing joints and back?

The life long effort to bring the gross and the subtle body to a oneness,

Not overcoming the longing for the all pure and the desire for the less pure.

Guruji's silent acceptance stands in the ashram like the winter sun in a dim, insecure sky:

Between white and bright, unreachable farness and an undeniable reality.

What will the spring bring?

Seeds without flowers and fruits, without delight and despair,

Seeds that cannot sprout anymore,
Exhausted in themselves, as attachment and the
desire to live burned long ago.

Even for a journey without return, preparations are
made.
Life will appear according to our belief in its reality.
You cannot avoid the intention to leave a note for
the children of the ashram, the cows, the vibrations
of a former life:
If, in case – if, in case ...
Only a formless emptiness will come back to hold
and spread blessings and strength to survive for the
ones who have to perform, to fulfill impatience.
In long nights of service massaging Guruji's feet, you
try to join His separating mind floating far away
behind the Himalayas, the Guru-land, the unknown
known, no Guru, no disciple, no Krishna, no Christ,
no bondage, no liberation.
Will you be strong and purified enough not to look
back and down and around, nor listen to the
innocent clinging of the child, the promises of Maya?
It seems your life energy to decide is dying out.
What to decide if the Lord of your life is turning the
eyes inwards, upwards, forever.

Like agents of another world, foreign devotees are
arriving to drive the heart of the ashram to Allahabad
– Prayag, leaving the three river children, Ganga,
Mandakini, and Alaknanda, behind.
A silent expectation of the divine will.

You hold your strength together:
Who knows? Certainly not you.

The journey is light, comfortable, with enjoyable
facilities.
Let all happen with a smile.
And Guruji agrees and smiles back.
You are allowed to sit close beside Guruji in the front
seat of the car,
A rare opportunity in all these thirty years of almost
never being physically separated from each other.
Driving straight roads to remember back and think
ahead of the unthinkable.
Twelve years ago, at the Allahabad Kumbha Mela,
Guruji's Guru left the body while sitting by the duni
fire, surrounded by His many disciples massaging the
holy feet, but unable to hold the fragile frame down
on earth.
You remember Dada Guruji[91] and the last afternoon
tea in those noble hands which led so many disciples
out of the wilderness;
The enlightened face with eyes glowing from the
other world that you had always seen shining
invisible over the Kumbha Mela.
You heard once more His divine voice "Narvadaji,
Narvadaji" which had appeared on the island in times
of deepest purification to save you from sinking too
far into hopelessness.
The time will come when all will belong to the past,

---

[91] The Guru of your Guru.

Memory will dissolve into an image of former life.
Twelve years back you had spun a mind gown of
blessings from Dada Guruji's love around you, to sail
you immune through the remaining night of Maya
that had still to be passed.
The next silent new moon will be the now and today,
and you will be unable to hold the falling leaf from
the tree of life, maybe even unable to join the fall.
What to inhale if the leaves of prana are no more?
How to protect yourself when the shadow will
disappear from the tree you were resting under?
The mother belongs to the child as a disciple belongs
to the Guru,
As death to life, or this to that.
Will Guruji take you with Him to the heavenly
ancestors to learn again the path to your causal
body?
Guruji awakens you one more time into the daily
illusion to accept what is the question of now and
here.
The journey moves on, as towards the end of
another life before emerging into the final one.
Guruji holds the secret,
Silent with no smile.
Never teaching how it would or should be – the
future will be your own faith, austerity, and vision.
Meditate, purify, love, and forget, to create a heaven
around and ahead.
Lower regions of consciousness will darken your life
through fear, anger, desires, and ignorance.
Guruji never made you enlightened or a renunciate,

showing more the opposite, to trap you into an eventual temptation, thereby awakening you to choose.

TWO

Kumbha Mela: Meeting of Heaven on Earth

In Allahabad, the divinity was already vibrating in high spirits,
Comfortable on earth, establishing a nakedness of truth and a spontaneous living with the bliss of renunciation.
Guruji enjoyed being received with sufficient respect and care.
The Guru family had reserved a tent for Babaji's disciples from far and near.
Guruji regained youth and immortality among the Sadhus, these embodied spirits who jokingly move from life to death.
Guruji was provided with enough means to distribute donations, always keeping His shy and modest image of Santosh:
Being nothing,
Having nothing,
Wanting nothing.
Our Guru-disciple relationship was fading away,
Two dried out bodies serving each other, even when the meaning had left long ago.
One soul united in the stillness of nowhere as a preparation to dissolve into being and non-being.

The crucial day of the silent new moon: the Royal
Bath where the kings and princes of heaven depict
the opposite of worldly rule: dancing, screaming,
fighting, naked joy, trampling down all bondage of
clichés, complexes, and habitual blindness.
Hidden corners of the worldly spectators tried to lift
themselves up toward the Light,
Where fear prevents all entry.
The inborn dream of the Indian soul: one day, one
life, all desires of the lower nature will integrate into
the ever-free.
Who will pay the price?
With faith, but weakness of sacrifice, they celebrate
the holy day, only to fall back into the hopelessness
of the victim.

The night before the bath vibrated in all pores and
corners of the divine play.
Guruji seemed to be hiding a strength and brilliance
which touches the danger line.
Nobody could sleep, even while pretending.
You remember the last Kumbha Mela when Guruji
allowed you and a Japanese Guru-brother to stay
awake in this night that turns all into Shiva energy.
An older heavenly friend had appeared, Ganesh Puri:
"Why not give Narvada the Kumbha Mela of Nasik?[92]"
(initiation of Nasik)
Guruji, as usual, knew better: silence was the

---

[92] The fourth site where the Kumbha Mela takes place, with a
majority of Vaishnav Sadhus, another monastic order, who
worship Lord Vishnu.

answer.

Your great Guru, who wonderfully heightened you by debasement!

Later on, when your meditative posture weakened around midnight you were sent to sleep, like children after ten o'clock.

A long way still to go towards the high life where sleep and non-sleep meet alike.

Defeated but not discouraged as usual: austerity is not for youngsters.

The law of "not this, not that" would prove itself.

Twelve years later: not much had changed in your eligibility.

This time the magic celestial night showed Guruji's yogic presence to many of His disciples.

The tent was packed with sleeping souls, all excited to wake into the heart of divine activities of the coming holy bath.

Two of them came back late from their endless wanderings from one tent of the supernatural to the next to witness the prevention of a disaster.

Before the most terrible sound "Fire!" could arise, a nightmare in all these close tents with duni fires, Guruji, whose fragility and inability to walk among obstacles was well known, had obviously flown from the back of the tent over all the sleepers' pots and bags, to the entry where the wind had driven the fire from the kitchen tent into the storehouse tent to feed on many tins of ghee, flour, sugar, and kerosene.

Guruji stood there to awaken the people to handle

the high flames.

Before the neighboring tents would panic, the fire was brought down and in a sigh of relief everybody went back to sleep with "God is great."

Guruji had taken His capacity from above to save the excited harmony of the Kumbha Mela night, taking all effort and discomfort into His departing body.

All strength to maintain was extinguished, risking the celebration of the day.

Silently you prayed, not allowed to nurse Guruji's bodily frame by massaging the trembling legs.

The morning activities of the thousands of dark beings, dressed into ash and flower garlands, fighting the cold with " Alak Bam![93]", further burdened Guruji's exhaustion, after the forgotten escape of the night.

Eventually Guruji gained back His lotus position and appeared positively pleased by the devotion of arriving disciples.

 "Narvadaji, go and have your bath."

Somebody had put the flower garland around your neck and, as in a trance, you bowed down to the paradise at Guruji's feet;

Leaving all unnecessary clothes, you were able to depart without question.

God must help you not to turn the fulfillment of your dreams into a reproach.

"You will take the nectar bath for Guruji's eternity."

Ganga! Yamuna! Saraswati!

---

[93] Chant of the seed mantra of Shiva.

The divine excitement all around made you proud
and humble enough to join your heavenly sisters and
brothers.

In all the Kumbha Melas of Haridwar and Allahabad,
you had danced the fairy dance of Cinderella,
Surrounded, and over-shadowed, and blessed by all
divinity from your meditation.

So much joy from your deepest Self must be the
Truth.

The more you disappeared into this forest of beings
of more soul than body, the closer you experienced
Guruji's celestial nature of the Avadhut, the ever-
free.

Had the time come to serve the Many?

You had always loved the One in your Guruji and the
Many was drawn into it to dissolve.

Were you now to recognize the One in All?

The happiness that originated from the confluence of
Ganga, Yamuna, and Saraswati (ida, pingala, and
sushumna) brought unknown liberating light and
brightness;

This time it sparkled not only for you, but in all of
these heavenly phantoms on earth living a dance
from unimaginable times ago.

Gange Hare! Narmade Hare!

Hare Hare Mahadev![94]

You felt in yourself the Ganga streaming down from
Shiva's dreadlocks.

Imaginations became invisible truth when you were

---

94 Praise to Ganga, Narmada, and the Supreme; mantras for
taking bath.

allowed to join all these souls screaming down from
life and life-long caves, temples, huts, and forest
heights to emerge from the one-sighted spirit into
the completeness of manifestation:
The wild purity of the naked frame body announcing
its origin: the light-beauty of the soul.
For moments nothing less than a worldly
completeness in its blissful simplicity,
An out-bursting joy of the children of God: the black,
the white, the old, the young, the fat and thin – one
smile of divine purity representing His Majesty on
earth.
Again it was there, that which you had felt since
childhood: the shy ecstasy when you dissolved
smaller than the idea of a cell into the divine body.
Jai Vishvanat! (Hail to the God of the Universe!)
The confluence of the rivers kissed your heart with
your own breath, which belonged to the rhythm of
this exceptional cosmic day.
The holy waters changed into nectar accepting unto
itself offerings of the Saints, giving the golden touch
generously to the profane.
With the devotional strength of a madman, you
carried Guruji's soul to gain His rebirth in the waters
of immortality.
A child was bargaining for one more Kumbha Mela in
Haridwar, with a stubbornness who knows its
weakness.
You shuddered in all this bliss, swallowed the nectar
to hurry back from where this celestial dream bath
had started:

Guruji's physical frame, His love and care and
knowing all but telling nothing.
Known and unknown moved by as on a train:
One sees all but catches nothing.
In the middle of the Kumbha Mela, in between all
Gurus and Seers: your Guruji, only your Guruji.
OM Shri Guruve Namah. (Prostration to the Guru.)
Awaiting you as thirty years back, the birth of your
spiritual life[95].
You should have hidden your crystal nectar-like
happiness better inside to pour your bliss out only
onto Guruji's feet.
For the mortal, only tears can wash His holy feet.
Live and live to die again in His True Name.

---

[95] One is said to be born anew when one meets the Guru.

THREE

Guruji's Mahasamadhi

"Narvadaji I am leaving this body not here, but in
Haridwar. Hasten to go back."
There it exploded, this hidden secret, always there
known and feared, but not accepted as reality.

The journey back was annoying for Guruji, bound to
uncomfortable externalities.
Guruji seemed to be torn between heaven and earth.
Arriving back in the ashram, the girls' innocent care
and love hold Guruji's body for another ten days,
Living life from a distance: a trembling void before
the great mystic change.
New and old disciples passed through the ashram,
waiting for a last darshan.
Guruji grew quiet listening to the calls from beyond,
which caused a pulling pain in the chest.
"Maybe an x-ray?" the world proposed.
Guruji adjusted to the proposal from far away.
Silent, but very, very united with another dimension,
Guru and disciple, the eternal mother and child drove
all the way, through the winter sun arousing the
colored beauty of Haridwar.
Our island passed by, we said goodbye to Mother
Ganga, the garden in Maya Puri (City of Illusion), and
Haridwar, the Gate to Heaven.
Guruji proved with the report that lungs and heart

were clean; the pain was caused by the unavoidable
farewell.
Guruji even allowed you to buy a walking stick for
His last journey – allowing you to join the pretext.
The life-long doctor friend was consulted but this
time it was Guruji who predicted the therapy by
finishing life at the earliest.

There was only reality and this truth gave strength
and clearness –
No thought, no sentiments for the past or future, no
question, and no answer remained.
"In half an hour complications will start. Narvadaji
will stay with me without any other duty."
Life manages its own way: clear and determined.
You had not eaten the whole day and were not
supposed to. Your perception had to be sensible and
light.
A long night to meet with death's hand was waiting
for you,
An even longer day of having lost everything,
And an endless time to be filled with what had lost
its sense.
There was no sign that Guruji was taking you with
Him, not for this life at least.
How could you be ready and prepared?
You were absolving something, still couldn't help
fighting against its surety and dreaming of the next.
Eyes heavy from unpoured tears,
The whole body too clumsy to pass the border.
You felt incapable, having learned again nothing to

be chosen for infinity.
Guruji seemed to have given up waiting for your
awakening any longer: Guruji's stillness and
indifference wanted only to separate, to escape –
leaving us in the search for explanations.
How admirably destiny takes its final steps –
Clear and simple –
Living the truth to be accepted for all.
The invisible presence that avoids reaction.
There you sat at Guruji's feet, all knowing, not
understanding, ending the day as ending one of the
many lives we had passed together.
The children on tiptoes tried to come near to hold
and press the head, embrace the hand, and massage
the legs.
Only for moments we were allowed to hold the frame
of the beloved father, mother, friend, the all for all.

Guruji's separateness drew wide circles and
distances: now it was not the time to show love and
care.
We had to be thrown out of the nest of Guruji's
presence designed to stand strong and hold
unshakable through faith and Guru-devotion against
the normal sea of distress and attacks.
Disciples, too fresh to know that they had become
the last ones to be chosen, came to fill the forgotten
treasure with tokens: a rosary, an inspiration out of
the final smoke, a neutrality to live centered in
oneself.
Fulfilling last responsibilities of the mortal frame,

Guruji left Himself by Himself.
You were allowed to stay near a shadow part of His
Self in the worldly plane.
One of these winter nights – full moon of the
auspicious Marg[96] month where shadows grab deep
into your heart, when every sound calls crystal clear
without any answer, this time void of any animal cry
to interfere with a Saint's departure from this world.
Usually the full moon was brightly celebrated around
Guruji but this time the devotees seemed to be told
to leave after the bath without accepting prasad[97].
"This is my last full moon, take you all care of the
cows and the ashram."
Who dared to take Guruji's words seriously thereby
accepting His passing away?
The heart knew well why mind and action did their
best to avoid this truth.

All of a sudden Guruji became strong – foreseeing
the day to follow – changed the two cloths He was
wearing, cleaned out all water of His body.
Guruji, with His only disciple child, set out for a
lonely night procession: from the duni fire to the cow
hall, passing the sleeping children, unnoticed. No
awakening – silently Guruji would leave the gross
body to remain all present, proud, unimpressive as
He had worked and meditated through His lifespan;
Guruji would remain all present, protecting and

---

[96] Mid-January - February month in the Hindu calendar.
[97] An offering made to God, then distributed, with God's blessing,
to devotees after worship.

guiding in His subtle form.
Returning from this weird walk, endless in its cold
determination, back to the fire:
A last union with the Supreme, the Light, and you
the individual.
The divine once again present in the middle of the
everyday world.

You sank back into the fire, the very last expression
of austerity.
Tomorrow another level of austerity will meet you.
Guruji left you with the fire and its dissolving power,
and disappeared inside.
In thirty years Guruji had tried to escape your
clinging devotion to make you live together in your
own being.
You couldn't give in or up, even now your body,
mind, and soul searched to hold to His Being.
Entering the room became entering a temple.
Guruji in lotus position was stretched up to
supernatural size; you felt immensely tiny when
bowing down to His soul.
Then singing up to His light, mantras, praise songs,
and the Aarti emerged from your being on their own.
The present turned into infinity.
Touching the ancient ties of the Rishis: Atri, Gautam,
Anasuya, Ahillya[98].
For seconds without time you left Guruji's body with
His spirit rising up into the nothingness of bliss, even

---

[98] Names of the ancient forefathers and their wives.

in infinity time holds you down in the finite.
Guruji had left His body, the body of your worship,
your own being, the place, the air around.
Your arms were holding a body, still breathing out
but without the spirit and you knew for the first time
you were alone in the world of darkness, coldness,
stones, and forms, and a moon, without connection.
Midnight had passed you
And death,
A void full of meaning.
The devotional songs and mantras had left your
memory, giving last company to the departing soul.
Guruji's whole life had been of seva to the world,
only one last minute to hold on His own was meant
to disappear, to dissolve:
All His life for others, one minute for Himself to die.
Hari OM tat Sat.

What had left, what remained?
All relation to yourself, to the all around, had become
lifeless, senseless, empty, and dreadful. This couldn't
be the end of the divine manifestation around you.
Where had your "I" gone?
Searching for yourself you lost the love for God, the
Guru, the Truth, by drowning into desperateness.
Remembering the name, the mantra, Guruji's soul
brought back the light, the meaning, and you
experienced that your real Self had left with your
Guru's prana.
Inseparable as you were and had always been, now
this union became the simplicity of existence, as an

unshakable truth.

You had become your Guru; your Guruji will go on living through you without suffering or limitation.

The inner light of your eyes had opened to see what had always been there.

Death of the body equals celebration of the soul.

Even in the body, in illusion and falsehood, you will live on in the soul which is your Guru's, so close to oneness with God.

Guruji's light had joined the heavenly abode – Shiva loka[99] – where you had always felt Guruji being the shadow in Shiva, the lord of lords.

At least Guruji had gotten freedom, liberation from unavoidable limitations.

An almost worldly, bodily happiness entered you, to feel Guruji being delivered from earthly bondage and shortages.

A new unknown kind of sacrifice: to worship the freedom of the soul and carrying on your shoulders the leftover burden of worldly responsibilities.

For a heavenly dream life you thought to hold Guruji alive through the strength of your devotion and faith,

Never daring to even imagine the hour Guruji could abandon His child disciple.

Now it was here: the present.

Devoid of any smoothing attributes: no sentiments, no fear, no anything, presence in its purest form.

And there was stillness:

---

[99] Realm; here, the region of Shiva's consciousness.

"Where the sun does not shine, nor the moon, nor
the stars,"
Self—illuminated, that light from which all shines —
In this void and darkness, in that aloneness, your
being was too raw to ask for a consoling light.
Incapable of forming a wish or thought, only to hold
this precious, auspicious, inexpressible moment
forever.
Guruji's abandoned frame had slightly leaned
towards you.
You were blessed to hold this mindless breathless
state.
No time, no movement, no sound,
Not life, not death.
Being in life's deepness —
To sink, to fall, to be as ever, forever.
Your first and final dream in these three decades of
guru life had been to sit and live in meditation by the
side of your Master, forgetting past and future, only
united in supreme consciousness.
Now this was reached in death at the beginning of a
new birth.
No body, no mind;
No you, no me;
No sound, no movement;
No sorrow, no delight:
The spirit and its manifestation;
The absolute before its contact with the elements,
ego, limitation.

Sita Ram, Radhe Sham[100]
Shiva – Shakti   Parvati – Ganesh.
The last communion of Guru and disciple:
Why could this supreme purity not last forever?
From midnight to dawn
Time of dissolution where the next illusion is already dreamt.

No conch will be blown at four o'clock,
The first time in thirty years that Guruji's datta conch will be missing,
The first sign of Guruji's physical absence, of being no more in this world.
The cows, the birds, the trees around, even Ganga Mata, might be astonished, asking what happened – where is Guruji's morning worship?
Life came back to your body.
Soon the day will come and its questions and sorrows.
You will stand alone.

The Spirit Lives On
Before the ashram would awake to the never-admitted reality, the mantra of OM Namah Shivaya, with origin-less force burst out of the stiffness and silence of your incomprehensiveness.
Hundreds and thousands of the mantras filled loudly every corner of the ashram, crept into the sleeping minds of Guruji's children,
And woke them up. Not wanting to accept the

---

[100] The union of the universal male and female.

meaning of this unusual morning prayer,
They came running, already weeping to surrender a
late devotion to what could no more be brought
back, making their life fall down like pigeons shot
dead in the middle of their happy flight.

When their emotions swept over you,
The first weakness of individuality grounded inside
you and while still holding your heavenly abode
through the mantra, streams of tears ran out of your
mind and heart and drawing you downwards from
the "neti neti[101]" realms of purity into facing
adjustment.
Not really tears of emotion or suffering, but the
physical reaction to the law of worldly illusion.
You will have to live what the divine wants you to.
Your dream will fade away to dissolve with Guruji's
soul in OM, OM Namah Shivaya.
What you will do? Your ego could not help asking
many times: will you be able to stop eating, sleeping,
talking, laughing, moving, breathing –
Searching endlessly with your mind in all heavens to
join the Lord of your life?
The real service to God is certainly not to live out
your fantasies and wishes, to die out of love, unable
to live without your god manifestation, but to submit,
humbly accepting your Kaliyug[102] birth.

---

[101] "Not this, not that" A (Vedic) philosophical expression of the
process of negation leading to the Ultimate Truth.
[102] There are four major ages of time, the current, and last, age
is the Kaliyug, the black age, when the dark forces of nature

You learn not until the experience.
The future of God's divine play seems like a surprise.
You fell through the thought which started to enter
your mind losing the sweet reality in Guruji's union.
"Mataji, stop the mantra singing!"
The children wanted to tear you onto their world's
side:
Soon you would give in and up, closing the secret of
your life and love forever into the softness of your
heart.
Soon they would win over and separate you from
your hold: Guruji's physical remains.

From all sides beings streamed in to bow their last
bow to the lord of death, the necessary end to all
that once began.
Everybody covered the loss with the law of survival
to carry the weight of responsibility left behind by
the departing soul.
Law of action, the law of life, and its overwhelming
power.
Management – handling the situation by the illusion
of what to do first and what next.
Guruji's children, yourself, and some faithful disciples
experienced a painful rebirth into higher stages of
consciousness.
Unknown sources of awareness started dawning.
Spiritual energy directly interfered into the children's
playful, superficial lives:

---

start playing an aggressive role in civilization.

"Awake and arise."
The young shoulders grew strong and responsible,
recognizing the real doership, separate of one's own
ego, still not different from the Self.
That day an established balance between life and
death was determined, to settle a start into the
unknown growth, to live the manifestation of the
divine spirit in the form of our Guru-Father-friend-
ancestor.
Time took its pace, and a long silent grayishness
moved around Guruji's stillness, sitting in the left-
behind-body, still expressing the last vibrations of
OM.

The worldly tradition told you to suffer the loss with
desolation, whereas your soul rejoiced, experiencing
the liberation from bondage, the flight back home to
its heavenly abode.
Could it have come true?
Had Guruji taken your soul with Him to the goal of
the unknown where no question is left, no answer to
be invented?
You could not stop seeing through Guruji's body,
which told of the beauty and peace of the soul,
expressing the truth of the manifestation even when
the divine in-dweller is missing.
Not different from your own bodily frame,
Empty and abandoned,
A dry leaf exposed to the merciless winds of nature.
The soul clung to see off its master's soul before the
time was ripe,

Allowed to accompany only the first part of the journey, then had to stay behind to weep into the unknown.

In the time of death the spirit is felt in its invisible beauty, clear, finally separate and independent of its bodily existence –
Drawing everybody around in its mysterious silence, beyond laughter and tears.
Bodies walking on tiptoe not to interfere with its subtle reality.
Moments dissolve into a less-ness.
Words and actions lose their meaning and determination.
Memory and plans are drawn, as ridiculous as bubbles.
OM Shanti OM OM.

Faithful devotees, who had sacrificed their labor to build up Guruji's Maya ashram, have now to prove their love and dig a tomb of their own devotion to bury their idol.
What a suffering to hasten a process that you never wanted to happen: to lose forever the compassion of the guru.
Last disciples arrive, fluttering around like birds who have lost their nest.

The Saints, the conquerors of death, arrive to praise the immortality of our real nature, to decorate the last wooden throne seat

To carry the illusion of the bodily remains as a victory
of the soul.
Smiling the message of wisdom, strong, shining the
light of lights, they skillfully perform the rights
according to the scriptures.
Your heavenly family has come to free you from
worldly weakness and sentimentalities, celebrating
the spirit, the message of life, in life.
Time hurries from one act to the next.
The ritual bath – Guruji once more makes the divine
play visible: seeming to be alive and near as ever,
while having departed as far as never.
Sitting in the one loincloth as years before, with the
same smile, familiar through each life a hanging
bridge between truth and illusions.

Before the body is dressed for the final procession, a
shadow of His universal soul escapes to hide around
your weeping limitation: from now on Guruji will live
in you.
Rejoice!
Who will weep if He is you and you are Him?
So Ham (He is me)
Ham So (I am Him)
Shivo Ham. (I am Shiva)

You are made to bid farewell – the world will carry
the wooden seat while the treasure remains with
you.
A farce – the inner Self alone is truth.
You sink into your own being that no longer belongs

to you.

Irrevocably, pregnant for your higher Self: the Guru inside.

No departure, but a secret birth.

Jai Jagadisha Hare! Hail to the Lord of the world!

The band plays professionally while Guruji is carried out of the ashram, colorful, beautiful with balloons and flowers.

Guruji's Ganga son matures under the heavenly burden, starting a blissful transformation into the main pillar of the ashram.

Guruji blessed all children with His immortality, staying alive in all of us.

Hari OM tat Sat. (God is Truth.)

Guruji, years ago, had foretold many a time to settle His Samadhi place[103] outside in the garden, facing the Ganga and the cows in front.

Only one day before, Ganga Puri was told to harvest baskets of turmeric from the very place that next day was to be dug out for Guruji's last abode.

The place looked destined, with its holy Bilva[104] tree, and fruit trees of mango, banana, pomegranate, lemon, and guava.

One little lemon tree had to sacrifice its youth to bend over the samadhi place contributing to the

---

[103] Tomb. The Samadhi Temple (tomb) of a Saint is alive with the spiritual power of the one who is buried there.

[104] Holy tree of Shiva, used in puja and in many medicines. Fruit is also known as Bael fruit or wood apple.

fairly tale-like mystery.

The procession carries Guruji, seated high,
Out of His ashram kingdom, down the Ganga road
Where shops close their windows so not to see the
undeniable.
Guruji's Santosh-life that never has allowed any
honor or reverence now is celebrated with silk and
flower garlands.

Ma Ganga is awaiting Her son to release the worldly
play of curse and blessing – a silent gate we all have
to go through: Shri Ram, Lord Krishna, the Buddha,
Shankara, the beggar and the king, the sinner and
the saint, any time, every second.
Guruji's duty is not yet fulfilled; He is not to be
allowed to dissolve and float away in the waters.
His small but lifelong devotional disciple family is
blessed to hold Guruji's presence at a permanent
altar shrine of a Samadhi Temple.
Guruji has to go on serving as a memorial, accepting
the hidden prayers and wishes.

The Lord of the ashram is carried back with trumpets
and drums to hold His Samadhi alive, deep in a cave
below the earth.
How speedily and industriously the worldly hands
work to accomplish their task.
Readily opening mother earth to receive and devour.
Ganga Puri has to dig his own grave to live again.
Cow dung, the water pot, the Gita, the mala, the

piece of bread, sandalwood powder, sugar, and salt.
Hare Hare Maha Dev.
(Praise to the Great God.)

The earth rains its heaviness to close another fairy
tale,
Burying a divine love and its manifestation.
Soon all the world will hurry away, you are waiting
for the night to come to sit on the earth and listen to
the story of birth and death –
To weep and smile, to hold the dream and forget
alike;
To walk away in the land without time and space or
tiredness;
To find again the light not to be seen,
The body not to be touched,
The song of no words –
From where there is no return.

Stop dreaming illusion!
Experience your reality.
Did your breath succumb when Guruji's final life
energy was flying home?
Could you blind your eyes to stop the world?
You are left behind –
Soon you will weep into another illusion, forced to
breathe and eat and talk,
Sing another song of the eternal longing of the soul.
Wake up!
Take bath and start again.
Time is so wonderfully crucial, rafting from one level

to the next.

It is time for the evening Aarti: praise the Lord and His victory over death and life.

"Ganga, blow the conch!" Everybody grasps this lifeline to save themselves from drowning.

An unknown source starts your survival and all alone you pray the hymns in a newly born voice and mind and courage.[105]

The deathlike shadow over the ashram is to be pierced, the emptiness to be filled and forced into a new creation.

Tears have to run - the chanting to be completed. Ganesha will help to cut the hindrances.

Om Dattatreya, Shiva, Ganga, Narmada, Saraswati... Hare Hare Maha Dev. [106]

The divine manifestation in mantras and chants will hold you alive, keep you grounded in truth, smiling the song of your heavenly home of oneness.

Thanksgivings of praise flow over you: your gods prevented you from falling into sentiments and suffering.

A seed has sprouted inside you to culture the flower of eternal happiness whose fragrance is devotion, its stem courage and faith,

The petals your service to beautify His glorious garden.

---

[105] Evening Aarti was not known - Mataji had to sing on her own until others learned.

[106] Deities that are worshipped in the puja with mantras and hymns.

The Aarti puja brought Guruji back into His unlimited
nature: no anger, no worry, no disease – all this had
died with the body.
Guruji started living in His blissful state as an
unshakable reality in the outer invention of loss and
dissolution.
"Narvadaji is not unhappy, no crying, no loneliness."
What is there to weep when Guruji never left us, is
living inside deeper and purer than ever before.
Every moment is filled with Guruji's presence, His
watchful look, His protective care.

Out of our inner being started to emerge a
continuous flow of spirituality: mantras and
meditation, prayers and hymns, as a never-ending
worship.
The breath of yoga filled us, a way of living in
devotion and pride throughout every day's action.
Discipline and purity prevented the rise of any
distraction or weakness through confusion,
desolation, or fear.
By meeting with death, one understands and solves
its mystery.
The devotees closed a circle of devotion around
Guruji's remaining spirit.
What before had been full of obstacles, loosened its
blockages to smooth our life.
We didn't dare to believe that Guruji's soul was
blessing us with such an easiness and inner
happiness.
Our natural inferiorities dissolved under Guruji's

compassion and forgiveness.

The time of purification and punishment seemed to change into a reward for all the hardships and austerities.

The destructive Shiva image transformed into the golden light of Sattva[107].

Bondage through relation with the body cleared into union with the formless.

Guruji was invisibly teaching us through the sacrifice of His body.

The children realized Guruji's greatness and spirituality – the father image dropped and purified into the vision of the great soul, the Mahatma.

The girls wondered how death could be so real, so above fearlessness.

Guruji, who had never shown signs of love and affection, now took care by entering their inner being and filled up their feeling of being abandoned with a sweet experience of divine love, deep, deep inside.

When the Guru loses His mortal form and becomes the divine expression from then onward one finds the formless Guru smiling from inside.

We all understood: when God takes, He gives a hundred times.

All the devotees gained, through the physical loss, a new height of awareness.

The whole ashram grew up into spirituality.

---

[107] Harmony.

The friend, the teacher, the relative, had now to be found in the scriptures, in the communication with the Indweller, in right living, right thought, right work.

Guruji's spirit had entered or never left the ashram as an unknown silence from beyond, which softened all hearts.

A smile was born unseen from the outer eye to give a source of energy to eventual hardships of the future.

The sixteen days of mourning passed in union with the departed soul.

Guruji's Samadhi tomb breathed a new life through the fresh-pasted cow dung, the never-extinguishing oil lamp, the roses and marigolds, and the continuous chanting of mantra garlands.

What other than inner peace and bliss will come to you when the voice of yourself sings the song of devotion and all eyes see through illusion to rest on truth, all organs sacrifice their functioning to the one remaining work for the happiness of all.

Adverse forces obviously lurking around the ashram found no entry as weakness, desolation, and fear remained absent in our oasis of Guru consciousness.

Guruji was constantly blessing us, which resulted in an unending awareness of the mind: the praise song in the voice and the ever-dissolving love in the heart.

Devotees, to share the spirit of the Guru, flew into the ashram from near and abroad.

Guruji's physical body, His smile and voice kept vibrating; the fire had left us but instead the Indweller of His being had entered each of us, disciple and devotee, according to the deepness of our relation with the Guru.

Highest teachings of detachment from the physical form were thus experienced.

The phenomena of death became a blessing.

The goal to realize the Self was taught to us in the most practical way.

Guruji's ashram became His spirit, the silence of truth that underlies all beings,

When happiness and suffering lose their separateness and live together like the tiger and the lamb.

This absence of emotions was experienced as a valuable treasure, the base for a liberated living.

Guruji Digambar:

The naked one, dressed by the four dimensions, the sky and the earth, out of nothingness, a luxury of abundance, started creating itself to celebrate Guruji's Samadhi.

Bandhara – a charitable feast!

Guruji had always avoided attracting attention or praise.

Now His invisible humbleness invited all divinity of smaller and bigger ashrams as well as the hidden Sadhus from the jungle on both sides of the Ganga.

The whole day: food contribution and prasad bags to be taken away.

Guruji had filled our pockets to donate from the full.
From where?
The wonder of all disciples:
Guruji is leaving nothing behind, but fulfilling all from
His abundance of compassion.
Guruji will remain the invisible lord, all of us serving
in devotion.

One last devotee-disciple, an artist, was told in a
vision/dream to paint Guruji's image in the yogic
posture to fill the empty place by the duni fire.
Nature, the holy vibration had taken over; we grew
into the silent witness resting in the peace of faith.

FOUR

Time to Fill the Void

Guru murti smaran nityam.
Guru namah sadah jape.
The form of the Guru is my memory.
The worship to the Guru is my japa.

The following years will create the ashram into a
center of harmony, inspiration, and creativity with
Guruji's blessing as substratum,
Guruji's Maya all around.
Every gesture, smile, and word became the Guru's
expression of compassion.
Even the walls and plants reflected their inner
happiness to contribute to Guruji's scenario.
Vishwa rupam - Vishwa deva:
The Lord is the form of the universe.
When the spirit becomes the form, the vision of God
disappears.
What remains is the golden light that transforms the
normal into a reliquary.
Soon life will survive on another time;
The transformation will bear fruits to be seen and
enjoyed by all.
You go on singing the Aarti, the chants of your life,
once sung with your Guru in the silence of dawns
and dusks, to reach the peaks of Shiva in the far
Himalayas:

"Guru Kedarnath Ji sada Shivam,
Kashi Vishwanath Ji Vishweshvaram."[108]
Or to wash, with the love of your heart, the holy feet
of Dattatreya.
You have to call and pray and praise all aloud to
reach Guruji's shadow as an attendant to the
Supreme lord.
Guruji, the farthest and nearest,
Praise, worship, and dissolve.
The one who knows can make millions believe.
The puja sings forth,
The mantra swings ahead,
Tears of love and joy flow and flow to join the ocean
of bliss.

The children watch your humble ecstasy, believe in
its truth and beauty and start the song of bhakti and
become happy in the loss of everything.
We will sing together, sing together…
Guruji's spirit will live and form us to its tune.
Our souls hold hands with Guruji's astral body.
There it is, that they were always looking for, the
real nature that lack of courage had resisted
revealing.
Changing their lives into what they had always been,
Finding peace in their divine heritage.
The song of the free is awakening.
Listen deep and know the way.

---

[108] "Praise to the Lord of Kedarnath and Vishwanath of Benares."

Ganga Puri finished his degree in science but the call
of the real had already been born inside him waiting
to burst and bear the fruits of light:
Yoga!
How it was that we had never thought about it.
All doors opened, expecting him, the son of a Yogi.
No question about his admission, long forgotten
father-souls were accepting him to offer the first
helping steps.
Soon the driving energy would lead him far ahead as
the bliss of yoga had not to be learned only to be
rediscovered.
Yogacharya[109], sweetening to the western-oriented
nervous mind,
Back to the vedic tradition,
Changing the black pants into white dhotis[110]
externally and internally.
The knowledge of the Vedic tradition opened its
treasures, and the Homa[111] fire hence on burned for
purification filling the atmosphere with its holy
mantras.

The younger girls in unquestioning astonishment
observed and witnessed the embracing flow of
spiritualization, listened to the initiating mantras,
promising awakening, purification, and divine
knowledge, from the Brahmans and Saints who

---

[109] Master Degree in Yoga Science.
[110] Indian traditional dress worn by Lord Krishna, a three to five
meter fine white cloth wrapped around the lower body.
[111] Ritual fire ceremony.

looked with a protecting eye over the ashram.
The finishing examinations became more a formality
to get prepared to drown and exalt in the ocean of
divine light.

Yourself remained clearly absorbed in what always
had been your inner nature.
Guruji's physical absence refined your gross
consciousness and reduced bodily activity and its
responsibility.
The loss of Guruji's earthly reality had awakened the
lotus flower of a constant smile, abiding in the Self,
which was your Guru, and Guruji became the Self in
its true appearance.

One year to reestablish the departed soul into the
Samadhi Temple with the Shiva lingam above, as
Guruji had foretold years ago:
"Worship the Shiva lingam on my Samadhi and no
harm for all of you."
For one year Guruji's light was to be contemplated
on, in the oil lamp burning day and night, spreading
hope, faith, and never ending love.
A brass lamp that Guruji presented to you years ago,
to use when the time would come.
Sitting in guru-consciousness, meditating, reading
the scriptures, chanting the prayers, witnessing the
flow of people coming, bowing down, and
disappearing.
Your heart remained with the light to smile in guru
confidence, endless peace dissolved in His eternal

presence,
So near, so far.

Sivaratri, the night of Shiva, will fall into the
mourning time as a cold statue without adornments,
a desert that vibrates the dream song of water.
We will meditate the flower back into the abandoned
garden!
One day again the scent will spread to revive the
bliss of former days.
Navratri, the nine fasting days of Durga, to weep out
your heart in the lap of the holy Mother, to dive deep
into her unending compassion.
The child in need,
To hide no cries,
To be told again the way to nowhere in yourself.
The priests sing and sing the holy verses and you
search to find what was never lost.
OM Shri Durgaye Namaha! Praise to the Mother of
the universe!

The birthdays of the Gods Ram and Krishna, the
enlightening day of the Buddha,
Passing celebrations, showers of blessings to hold
your abandoned soul in love and care to breathe in
never disappearing unity.
Nights of sitting on Guruji's Samadhi grave to listen
into the dark and establish the light that is always
there.
The nothing, the normal, the every day rhythm dress
up into the divine Lila of ancient times to be repeated

again and again.

Death eternal, always present – never understood.

The mystery that weaves life's threads of illusion into the emblem of truth and fearlessness.

The rains will wash the remaining sentiments away and clear for the morning to come to renew awakening.

Live the mission;

Fulfill your debts.

Invest a new sacrifice for times to come.

Without beginning and end, the elements around are observing our breath to search deep inside to listen to the voice that is always there to guide you out of the darkness.

The whole ashram stands still for us to follow the Guru in the love of the heart:

The tears of the mind,

The dreams of the night.

The world will come again: a fresh idea, unknown from before, an energy to follow, a call that the loneliness has to change into universal friendship.

The one Guru had been All for us, now the All became a oneness and this oneness awakened to a new happiness:

A higher level of independent knowledge, experience and bliss.

The truth will start happening to emerge from the inside.

Wonderful –
Life had conquered,
Opened untouched doors of celebration where you
dance with your own Self.
We all felt the same silent grace
Born on death
To start a work immortal.
What happened?
Darkness was lifted
Confusion dispelled
Anger sweetened
Longings fulfilled.

In the dawn of life
All is expansion,
Plurality,
Heights and breadths.
What remains toward the end,
The white pages of the void,
Are calling to eliminate past and future.

Five

Work to Establish What Has Died

Building the Samadhi Temple
"The rainy season is over. You don't start to build Guruji's Samadhi Temple?"
A Saint arrived to wake us from soft dreams to live in sweet memories.
Arise to sing a new song of love.

The first year, that taught us how to survive through a prana that had left, was closing.
Before we knew what was happening, faster than our individual inertness, the Divine will started the work: from all sides Saints, priests, workers, designers, and traders moved into the ashram to help advise and plan.
Where the temple over Guruji's Samadhi was designed to stand, the starting ritual of the earth worship (Bhumi puja) was performed.
Yourself had the vision of a round temple, which was changed into the auspicious eight corner design.
This eight angle inspired Ganga Puri to design in the sand with his toe, eight columns around the predicted lingam, crowned by a dome to unite all eight corners into one trident on top.
That was the only design to enable a construction to

complete its first end in the inauguration of the Shiva
lingam at Guruji's first samadhi anniversary.
In less than a quarter of a year, through a dream-like
digging, forming, and continual improvement,
obeying an inner order and determination,
The construction was accomplished.
Was Guruji's spirit building His own Samadhi Temple?
The masoners and laborers worked in smiles and
overtime.
All disciples joined the work to give a late service to
their Guru.

A Muslim expert in the building of domes introduced
himself. Building the dome, he experienced an
unknown power directing his work,
Not according to a fixed design, but he saw his
hands building up a vision to unknown heights.
Forgetting lunch and sunset, he went on working in
the moonlight after the workers had all left.
"I don't know what is going on, only that I have to
go on, higher up than ever planned."
Everybody was wondering where the little Samadhi
Temple was going to grow.
The workers couldn't help abandoning their work as
the dome overloaded the first eight ground columns
creating a swaying impression.
We held our breath.
This miraculous, blessed construction could fall or
crumble?
Impossible! Defeat or failure of divine energy?
Your night meditation wanted to hold up and support

your Guru Memorial.

So quickly one gets trapped into beauty, happiness, and success, but losing the blessing's source.

A compassionate reminder only: still a chance to stabilize through another round of eight supporting columns – the Samadhi ground breathed in relief.

A nothingness of time before the anniversary:
Guruji's artist disciple arrived to prove a blessing of inspiration in order to establish Guruji's mortal form in concrete, enlivening His soul through sand and water.

To enjoy paradise is to enjoy that simplicity and easiness throughout, in which all problems and difficulties lose their importance.

What remains is a divine flow in which all moves and smiles –

And smiles and moves.

Shiva is Brought Home

Lord Shiva's presence will be established through a lingam stone "Narmadeshwara" from Omkareshwara[112].

A present for your birthday: verily another birth falling together with Guruji's first death anniversary.

The Goddess' energy awakens to meet the Lord established in the symbol, and to carry it high up: from now on this is the God your Lord.

---

[112] These Shiva lingams come from the Narmada River, one of the seven sacred holy places of pilgrimage in India. Omkareshwara is an island in the Narmada River.

Faith, bliss, and devotion, and you dance on the clouds of heaven.

Lord Shiva doesn't mind becoming Narmada so that Narmada can become the Lord.
The Narmada inside you knows no end of rejoicing.
Had Guruji to die to fulfill your dreams?
The doors of heaven are wide open to make you understand that worldly limitations only stop you from experiencing enlightenment.

Three women disciples – yourself one among them – will travel to Omkareshwara to bathe the lingam manifestation in the waves of Narmada.
You will go. For the first time you travel far away, to meet your Guru as the Lord of here and there and everywhere.
The bliss of your soul is truth where everything dissolves into the final peace of your Guru.
You see yourself easily departing from Guruji's "firebreath" (the duni) to travel in Guru's light towards Omkareshwara.
No leaving, no arriving:
Just experiencing the divine smile's protection and affection.

Bowing down to the Jyotir Lingams[113] feels like starting a new admission into the High Lord where

---

[113] Self-created, illuminated stone manifestations of Lord Shiva. There are twelve in India, one in Omkareshwar, and another nearby.

Guruji could reveal Himself in the subtler form of
devotional manifestation.
Gange Hare, Narmade Hare
Half a life's call and prayer:
There She comes down from Amarkant[114]
To melt you down towards the sea.
Just She, the celestial beauty, a presence of bliss and
grace, to make one forget the search for any other.

We three elderly damsels,
Divinized through our vision,
Walk with crystal feet on paradise ground –
Nymphs in the disguise of mortal grossness attending
to the Lord of Omkar.
Heaven is truly the divine presence.
Encircling the Supreme to bow down to His feet,
Where is the beginning of that which has no end?
The Omkar island embraces us as the absolute of
that which Guruji is an omnipresent part.
The whole world is seen in a glimpse of the divine
body.
Your devotion dissolves into the clear dried blueness
of the Narmada River to encircle the Lord eternally in
OM Namah Shivaya.
Our minds walk on tiptoes over Lord Shiva's island
body Omkareshwara, diving deep into the waves of
Narmada to find the heavenly sister, the ideal image
of ourselves.

---

[114] Source of the Narmada River, site of immortality.

Among hundreds of Shiva lingams, the friend inside
the oracle of your past and future, there you see His
straight omnipresence:
A stone of Shiva's smile, the omniscient.
The attraction of your heart pulls you toward Him to
surrender once more to the form of the formless:
The six-inch high majesty from the stone's inner
being, the omnipotent eye, is glowing in a reddish
circle to absorb all and forever.
The fontanel in the crown of the stone marks the
eternal opening for our never-ending waters of
devotional tears, desires, and wishes[115].
A subtle foam of jatta design will allow the dreams to
flow into His unmanifested infinity.
Lord Shiva as Narmadeshwara allows us to pay for
His holiness that has no limitation.
Truly God is the incarnation of His creation's faith
and surrender.
Jyotir lingam, the lingam of supreme light,
Omkareshwara, the primordial bliss, will grant the
holy touch to give birth to a divine offspring to be
taken home as prasad.
A sacred heaviness of forty-five kilos is carried home,
hanging from a stick not allowed to touch the ground
until the destination is reached:
Guruji's Samadhi Temple in our Santosh Puri Ashram.

A heavenly Bandhara, Guruji's first anniversary; the
inauguration of the Samadhi Temple, the

---

[115] In puja for the Shiva lingam, water is poured continually over
the crown.

Narmadeshwara lingam, and Guruji's concrete statue,
Shining, smiling, blessing, knowing, watching,
supervising all while watching with closed eyes.
Hundreds of Saints and bhaktas could be given
prasad by the spirit of a simple renunciate continuing
serving from the fullness, just through the eternal
mantra of "Shiva Shiva," the cow seva, and the
Atman seva.

New Growth and Change
Guruji's so-called absence was for everybody
transformed into a manifestation of bliss.
Guruji's spirit entered faraway hidden corners to
enable a continuous flow of construction for years
under the surveillance of Guruji's chosen instrument
of expression.
What Guruji had never allowed to happen, now
started to be revealed through His naturally born
disciple:
Ganga Puri's cool and steady determination changed
the outlook of the ashram – beautifully decorated
facilities, a simple luxury,
Devotion and spirituality grew to express Guruji's
understatement and basic truthfulness towards the
roots of religion: brotherhood, compassion, and
desirelessness.
Your own heart softened and rejoiced to witness a
visible manifestation of truthfulness, devotion, and
yogic renouncement.

Guruji's renouncement broke open into a sharing

expression like springtime colors melt the winter ice
to enjoy the scent of dance and laughter.

The cows and their seva had fertilized a ground for
inspiration and spiritualization.
The cowshed inside the ashram gave way for a
meditation hall, retreat rooms, and a library. Where
the cows had ruminated like the repetition of the
cosmic rhythm, seekers of truth will meditate to
reach back to our inborn wisdom.
Where grass and hay had been stored,
Annapurna's[116] prasad will be served to nourish and
strengthen the spiritual body.
The cows, in their indestructible Santosh, will follow
Guruji's mortal frame outside the ashram toward the
holy Ganga; in front of Guruji's Samadhi Temple they
will continue the song of elementary peace and
forbearance.

Incredible – Guruji allowed us to live the expression
of austerity fulfilling the promise to let the ashram
flourish and to prevent all possible difficulties
through the performance of daily puja at Guruji's
Samadhi Temple.
Akand jyoti – the ever burning light at His tomb –
became the prana, the life energy, of the ashram.
Daily Aarti puja, Yoga sadhana, an increasing interest
and surrender of foreign aspirants, the sharing of the
scriptures ("The Bhagavad Gita," "Patanjali's Yoga

---

[116] Hindu goddess of food and cooking.

Sutras"), all established a living presence of divine energy.

With tears in our eyes, we witnessed that neither our activity nor intelligence were providing the bliss and peace, but Guruji's soul that had joined the heavenly spirits was now living in our hearts as around us in the elements.

A blessing of nature's service in the holy tulsi plant; the tree gods of Banyan, Peepul, Neem, and Bilva[117], the fruit tress of mango, lichee, banana, guava, pomegranate, and jack fruit joined the celestial garden.
As the life stream of our ashram body, Ma Ganga blessed us with divine vision to see our normal worldly life as a gift from heaven.
One breath awareness,
A total transformation from the darkness of illusion to the light of wisdom:
Constant prayers, sadhana, svadhyaya[118], all seemed to hold even a shadow of negative energy away.
You wonder how Guruji's often angry teachings could change into such a bluish gentle morning breeze.

---

117 Four holy trees: Banyan, Peepul (the holy fig tree - tree of eternal life), Neem, and Bilva.
[118] Spiritual studies.

SIX

Final Living Sacrament

Less Than Less
All alone with a heavy body, the spirit, your lord of prana, abandoned you only to guide you to follow after.
The way through the drought to the valley of the golden rose,
Emptying out to the nothing left, where you will have to swim in an ocean, where even the desire of bliss has dried out.
You find yourself forlorn:
Where to hold on when you destroyed all supports?
No smile, no tear
No bliss, no fear
Following the path into your own end.
Far away
In the near inside
A barren happiness will bear a fruit that shines without light.
Shades of colors from a screen long forgotten at the bottom of a womb,
Too full to add to or to reduce.

Since Guruji's samadhi you slowly lose interest to eat cereals, to support the prana of Kaliyug[119], instead to

---

[119] In Kaliyug, the age of darkness, grains and cereals are the

live on Guruji's spirit alone, only to survive on His
remembrance, only to die in His rebirth.
Even the remaining fruit and milk weigh heavy on
your dream flight where limitations chant the song of
freedom.
Less food, less words, less study, less comfort – less
than less to try once more and again to walk the
edge of a self-constructed sword.
A dark bounding dance with the higher Self.
Could you give up, to live and breathe and weep the
soul's primordial glance – His eternal presence?

Amazing how heavy life and past are pulling you
down.
Time will raft you to feel lofty enough to enjoy the
earth element as you embrace the higher spheres.

Ujjain
A first breakout from the ashram harmony to run into
a jungle of heavenly spirits: the Kumbha Mela at
Ujjain.
Unable to understand yourself, how could you
explain it to your children?
Time will show where they belong.
You cannot deny the strong call of your soul:
To join the brother and sister souls of ash and
austerity.
An original expansion beyond time and reason.
Guruji's Shiva energy is everywhere,
Leading into another incarnation on a higher level of

life-supporting energy.

Sainthood.
The exciting vibration when vision becomes
manifested,
No words to tell, no body any longer to be
experienced.
A presence beyond world: finally a reality that is
visible without the illusion of form.
That could be why one gets so drawn into the bliss
of the Kumbha Mela, which got its name from the
highest yogic practice of Kumbhaka, Kebala
Pranayama[120]:
Union in an everlasting retention with Shiva, the
lingam, the pure utmost energy.

With a group of twelve from the ashram you enter
the Guru family.
Something irresistible has been driving you.
All of a sudden you cannot hold any more the last
remaining wish of over thirty years,
A prayer without praying in the middle of the Mela,
You ask without a question.
What more is there to achieve if the normal world
had already changed into a heaven, a Baba-Sadhu
into Lord Shiva, a river into the holy Ganga, your
limited soul in to the Supreme Atman?
Against all ridiculousness, after half a life of imposed
and lived sannyasa,
You bow down again, as if for the first time, and ask
for initiation that had long ago taken place.

---

[120] Kumbhaka Pranayama is deliberate retention of the breath; in
Kebala Pranayama one transcends inhaling and exhaling.

A shower of bliss for your little devotional soul,
invisible for the outer world.
The shaving, two cloths, the single rudraksh seed,
the mantra, the Guru and the Guru's Guru, all had
been given to you in the subtle heavenly way.

"After decades of driving, you ask for a license."
All seemed surprised and wondered about its
necessity.
"We all thought you had been initiated long ago."
"Yes, sure --"
You almost give in; you will go on staying close to
God as before.
You couldn't help but to express this little desire from
your Guru-disciple life –
And now withdraw back and let the divine will
happen.
You even are ready to go back to the ashram before
the initiation day to accept your responsibilities.

"Narvadaji - tomorrow six o'clock."
One of Guruji's younger brothers stands to his
promise:
"If the wish of Samskara[121] awakened in her, it
should be fulfilled on the basis of her full-hearted
seva to our Guru brother and the Juna Akhara[122], as

---

[121] Initiation where all ones former karmas are eliminated.
Sadhu receives the death sacrament so he can now die
anywhere and anytime – body is purified and will go to heaven.
[122] One of the seven monastic orders created by Shankaracharya
(a figure akin to the Pope in Christianity).

everybody knows."
Your whole being becomes one breath of truth –
tomorrow will be the greatest day of your life for
lives.

A last phone to your children turns into a test, a
challenge from the voice of attachment to hold you
back from a final step that had long ago been taken.
The children unfortunately are shocked;
They see their mother disappearing into the jungle
mountain cave or maybe even separating from them
and Babaji to renounce into another family.
Undoubtedly a blow to your late heavenly
excitement.
Will your life-long endeavor become fruitless: to
achieve a renunciate life in devotion while
maintaining an indifferent service to your own
children?
Will you fall back from a spiritual flight into the lower
level of attachment and responsibility?

Since the beginning of living the end of a former
karma, you had always been free of attachment;
Now, you feel like renouncing the renouncement,
following the highest dharma not to hurt anybody's
feelings.
The shadow, thrown by the loneliness of a habitual
ego, can't conquer a truth deep from your inside: the
unshaken faith in the heritage of sannyasa
overcomes a potential obstacle,
And truth once more shows courage and bliss

through all the pores of your being.
To decide for the Supreme Path can never bring
suffering to anybody, certainly not to your children.
Your brave decision for an enlightening end state can
only bring uplifting and purifying transformation.

And so it will be.
In an innocent independency of all and everything,
you march your way towards an end of your
samskaras[123].
Once more and forever, the aging, ever-young bride
of the Lord!
What a beauty and grace to walk on the other shore,
separated from bondage, attachment, and illusion,
dressed in truth and a smile of the one who loves
nothing more than the unknowable.

At the day's end no hidden samskaras will be able to
claim possession, but are cooled away in the rivers of
ambrosia.
The one hundred and eight baths and the
accompanying mantras awaken your consciousness,
Transforming you from the gross body into a
heavenly but still unsubtle plane representing the
earth and water elements of the two root chakras
(muladhara and svadisthana)[124]. The Homa fire

---

[123] The impressions of past actions stored in the subtle body and
carried forward through lifetimes until balanced or erased.
[124] There are many centers or nexus of consciousness-energy in
the subtle body. Six main ones run along the sushumna channel
in the spine. Root chakras are the two lowest centers.

places, sparkling in all directions, are for the final
purification.

The walk through the fire of manipura chakra (navel)
is effortless and light;

You are attracted by the never-ending call of the two
higher centers: air of anahata chakra (heart) and
space/ether of vishuddhi chakra (throat).

Twenty-four hours of uninterrupted
OM Namah Shivaya mantra

Expands your heart center to the ends of the world.

The heart smiles in tears and love: undefeatable by
any obstacle.

Bondage is overcome, transforming into overall bliss
of the lowest into the highest.

Midnight is near: the end of a journey of a million of
lives in one day.

The mantra has proved its magic and can dissolve
into the silence of akasha, the ether element.

You are not yet allowed to give up the physical path
of manifestation;

Karma, the last japa, has to go on – one more hurdle
to be conquered.

Five minutes before twelve,
The Vijai Homa fires (Victory over death!) are
burning the final samskaras.

Why did you open your eyes to the world around?

Even a heavenly saintly world is a world: you see
your Guruji's brother being called to discuss
Narvadaji's eligibility for this final initiation.

No foreigners appreciated!

Forces want to deny the midnight Mahavakya
mantra[125].
The attachment of vishuddhi (throat) chakra: still a
victim to obstacles called success or failure.

You faint back into your invisible marriage with the
Lord as always when defense reaches its peak.
There is no higher truth than the Lord: even in a
deepest fall, the divine hold won't loosen.
You forget all in surrender to the nowhere,
To that indestructible power of the Self:
The greatest obstacle, the mind, disappears into
nonexistence.
The silence of nowhere-land, no fears nor
distractions open your sensual eyes.
A time without present or past makes you the seer of
the oneness of the outer and the inner: ajna chakra's
(third eye) kingdom, the abode from where no way
leads back.
The heavenly simplicity of the same in the form or
the formless.

Darshan!
The Acharya of vedic knowledge has invisibly arrived.
You bow down to the divine form of the Sat Guru[126]
whose light and wisdom
United you into a new unbroken depth with your root
Guru.
Final obstacles that separated you from the form of

---

[125] The four great Vedic mantras.
[126] Perfect Master.

the Universal Guru are removed:
A last purification through the light of oneness,
From tamas to sattva and beyond:

Chanting the name of Shiva you meet Lord Krishna.
When the Lord lived on earth, it must have been like
this – bliss and lightness all around everywhere,
Where Shiva becomes Krishna, the enjoyer of final
purity.

Once the sky clears and the sun of sattva appears,
you are no more bound even to bow down:
Purity speaks for itself;
Devotion needs no humbling.
Eventual shadows of attachment are easily overcome
as the light allows no darkness.
Real nature demands no opposite.
An immense improvement.
An achievement:
The struggling breath brought you to the top of the
hill to experience the above all around,
To reach the abode from where there is no return.
The forward and backward has disappeared –
It seems forever.
Your life will become a Nirvana Stotram[127]:
"No Guru – no disciple.
No bondage – no liberation.
No birth – no death.
No body – no spirit."

---

[127] Praise Song of the Soul: Famous hymn of Adishankara (Hindu
sage, born 788 CE, first Shankaracharya).

Hari Om tat Sat.

Kumbha Mela is happening –
The vessel of nectar flows over and bathes your
inner being.
The bliss of ajna chakra: the seer and the seen are
inseparable.
The All has given your heart the golden touch. You
become Him.
Tat twam asi
Aham Brahmasmi.
I am That.
So Ham, Shivo Ham.
He is me. I am Shiva.
The day's end of eternity is present –
In the middle of the same world, a glimpse of
infinity.
Dressed in the bondage of form and time, your soul
is oneness with all souls around, it is carrying the
limitation of the body in unawareness.
Behind the High Priest the chosen souls are
following,
Renouncement bears its fruits.

A last necessity of the Shipra[128] bath, and,
Quivering and newborn, we are awaiting the divine
mission.
Words of knowledge have changed into awareness.
Wisdom of what is beyond all is being and becoming

---

[128] Holy river of Ujjain.

energy in a final smile of light: sahasrara (highest center).

The thousand petals are the whole creation, gross and subtle.

Separation cannot exist.

You will carry the lotus forever on the top of your head to give the reason for your eternal smile.

Before you would have danced and rejoiced, now you hold the treasure like the most natural gift,

Passing loss and gain,

Your inborn heritage.

Shadows of shaved souls find their way back to their heavenly families' sleeping bodies of conscious souls.

To sink into an embracing deep sleep of a samadhi, the harmony of the unknown beyond the you

And me

In Thee.

It is done – a thousand layers of consciousness have reached one thousand and one.

The one jump out of the more than normal.

The dream of the individual soul to finally dissolve the dreams of dreams, carrying the security of the vedic thought.

The Mahavakya is the support of your being:

I am That;

That Thou art;

I am Brahman;

Wisdom is Brahman.

The most miraculous death from which you escape as smoothly as leaving one layer behind

Only to realize the higher one shining from beyond.
Austerity, struggle, and endless endeavor have lost
their grossness to establish the good in its subtle
eternal form.
By searching, the other you is united in yourself.
Guruji everywhere has become yourself no-where.
Guruji even loses His limiting individuality and
transforms into the saintly body of the Kumbha Mela.
You understand why Guruji never wanted to be
made a personal Guru, the Enlightened One, to make
you understand the Guru-light down to the lowest
core of existence.

Om Namah Shivaya.
Om Sri Guruve namah.
Too simple to be recognized
The dream of the dreams, in the dream of the
dream, after the dream to be dreamed. ...

Eternal Mahamaya was born without being born.
You slip into your soul-being to dance divine ecstasy,
Too fine to be seen,
Too near to be denied.
The lowest part of infinity is the enlightened one for
the finite.
Before you might have felt the bliss of the heart –
Now bliss itself is you.

What remains?
In your life remains the invisible vastness of the universe, the familiarity is your saintly family.
A last longing holds you alive: to join the rays of the sun to give equally warmth, growth, and support to the hidden dark corners of existence.
The god inside will make you be, to give a smile, to embrace with the breath of eternal love.
What remains?
To dissolve with all your pores and cells into divine love.
The soul will see with the eyes, and embrace and caress the smooth, the harsh.
The soul's motherly care will feed and please in your hand actions.
The wisdom of the Supreme will vibrate in the silence of your words.
The little garden place of your life will blossom again to create flowers of love to fade away while leaving a seed of indestructible devotion.
With open eyes, you have passed away long ago.

Amen
Ameen[129]
Om

---

[129] Islamic form of Amen.

Glossary

Aarti   Fire worship involving the waving of lights and incense before a Saint, idol, or the holy Ganga. (see also puja)

Akhara   There are seven monastic orders created by Shankar-acharya (a figure akin to the Pope in Christianity); Santosh Puri a member of the Juna Akhara.

Atman   Soul, true innermost Self of everything; Paramatman.

Avadhut   An enlightened being who has risen above body-consciousness, duality, and worldly concerns.

Baba(ji)   Term of affection for a holy man.

Banares   Holy city of Lord Shiva.

Bandhara   Celebration

Banyan Tree   Kind of fig tree, respected as holy, having long air roots hanging down like dreadlocks of Lord Shiva.

Bhakti   Devotion. Bhakti yoga is Union with God through the path of complete devotion.

Bilva Tree   Holy tree of Shiva, used in puja and in many medicines. Fruit is also known as Bael fruit or wood apple.

Chakra   There are many centers of energy - consciousness in the subtle body. Six main ones run along the sushumna channel in the spine, from the pelvic floor to the crown of the head: muladhara (root), svadisthana (tailbone), manipura (navel), anahata (heart), vishuddhi (throat), and ajna (third eye).

Darshan   Sight; vision of the divine, of Truth. Being in the presence of a great being.

Dattatreya   One of the twenty-four incarnations of Vishnu, a deity with three heads symbolizing Brahma, Vishnu, and Shiva.

Dharma (dharma) Living in accordance with Divine will; Law of righteousness. The highest dharma is to live one's true nature.

Dharmsala   Charitable food and shelter for pilgrims.

Duni   Sacred fireplace of the Sadhu, the fire is never allowed to burn out.

Fakir   A Sufi term: an Enlightened One, One who loves God and sacrifices all for God. Like Hindu Sadhu, renounces family, wealth, physical comforts.

Ganga Mata   The Mother, Her Divine form in the Ganga river.

Ghats   Stone steps providing access to India's rivers in many cities; places for bathing and worship.

Ghee   Purified butter

Guru   One who leads from darkness to light, a realized/liberated being.

Homa fire   Ritual fire ceremony. The Vijai Homa fire is the Last Sacrament given to renouncing Sadhus.

Japa   Repetition of a mantra using a mala/rosary.

Jattas   Matted hair, dreadlocks.

Karma   Law of cause and effect, past actions and lives have their consequences in the future. (see also parabdha karma)

Karma Sannyasa Renouncement in action.

Kumbha Mela   A sacred Hindu pilgrimage that takes place at the following four locations of India every twelve years: Allahabad-Prayag, Haridwar, Ujjain, and Nasik. Saints, Sadhus, and pilgrims make up the largest gathering of humanity in the world.

Lila   The divine play, sometimes referring to the Mother Herself.

Lingam   The symbol of the unmanifested form of Shiva (a statue of Shiva is the manifested form).

Mahant Heir, caretaker of the Ashram.

Mahasamadhi Conscious state of the soul at the time of leaving the body; conscious death.

Mantra A series of seed sounds, syllables whose meaning is beyond the "word," leads one to the Reality itself. Repeated for meditation and chanting or for some specific effect.

Mahamaya The Great Illusion, Lakshmi, the Goddess Herself, the Force that veils the Truth, that presents the temporary and unreal as real and everlasting.

Maya Illusion: everything of the manifest world is illusion in Vedic philosophy. Maya is the limited, purely physical and mental reality in which our everyday consciousness has become entangled, a veiling of the true, unitary Self.

Naga Babas Ascetics, followers of Shiva, who are "clothed in space" (naked) and covered in ashes (symbolic of the temporary nature of the physical body).

Neem Tree Tree known for its bitter taste and healing qualities.

OM Namah Shivaya Mantra meaning Salutations to Shiva, the Formless One.

OM Namo Narayan Mantra meaning I bow to the Divine in everyone.

Parabdha karma Accumulated past actions, the fruits of which are experienced now and cannot be erased.

Prana Universal life energy, the life force that infuses all beings, all manifestation.

Prasad Offering made to God, then distributed, with God's blessing, to devotees after worship.

Puja   Worship of the Divine through invocations, prayers, songs, and rituals.

Rishis   The wise Enlightened forefathers of Vedic (Indian spiritual) Tradition

Rudraksh   The seed of the holy Rudraksh Tree used in malas/rosaries and in initiation to Sannyas; believed to the be tears of Shiva.

Sadhana   Spiritual practices.

Sadhu   Ascetics who have taken a vow of renunciation and are dedicated to achieving liberation through meditation and contemplation of God.

Samadhi   A state of union with God, achieved through meditation.

Samadhi Temple Tomb of a Saint, which is charged with the spiritual power of the Saint buried there.

Samsara   The soul's cycle of birth, mutability, death and rebirth.

Samskara   The impressions of past actions stored in the subtle body and carried forward through lifetimes until balanced or erased.

Sannyasi   One who has taken a formal vow (Sannyas) of renunciation and seeks liberation from reincarnation through meditation and prayer.

Santosh   Contentment, Self-sufficiency.

Sattva   One of the three gunas (qualities of nature): harmony, light, and purity.

Seva   Selfless service.

Shanti   Peace

Svadhyaya   Spiritual studies.

Tamas   Tamas is one of the three gunas (qualities of nature): the quality of darkness, ignorance, and inertia. Tamasic is descriptive of tamas.

Tapasya   Austerities, repentance performed with the aim of purification of mind and body

About The Author: Narvada Puri

In 1969, a twenty-four year old German girl left everyone and everything behind to hitchhike to India to find meaning and purpose of life. She came with only a sleeping bag, a shawl, a flute, and a copy of the "I Ching." A year later she found her Guru, a Naga Baba, living on a small island in the Ganga north of Haridwar.

Her heart recognized Him immediately, and there she stayed to be reborn through strenuous spiritual austerities, serving the holy cows, meditating by the Ganga – and through the grace of her Guru. The first year she spoke no words except "Om Namah Shivaya." The first ten years her body nearly died (several times), but a remarkable inner strength and absolute faith in her Guru kept her alive and on the path.

Eventually, she learned Hindi and Sanskrit, married her Guru, and they had three children: Ganga, Mandakini, and Alaknanda. Her sister and Mother also came and took initiation from Babaji. Together Babaji and Mataji founded Santosh Puri Ashram. Babaji took Mahasamadhi in 2001.

Now Narvada Puri and the three children run Santosh Puri Ashram, living, teaching, and doing sadhana.

About Santosh Puri Ashram

Santosh Puri Ashram was founded by Baba Santosh
Puri in 1978 along the Ganga, on the historical
footpath from Haridwar to Badrinath. Starting from a
raw piece of land, Babaji built an ashram that, in
addition to the duni place and original cow spaces,
now houses 25 people, plus dogs and cows, and
includes a meditation hall, a dining hall, and a library.
They also have gardens to grow vegetables, dal, and
fruits. They even create their own "biogas" from the
cow dung, which is used to cook tea and food in the
ashram kitchen.

A spiritual oasis, away from the distracting world of
desires, the ashram is life in simplicity and
truthfulness. Visitors can come for any of the formal
courses offered year-round, or for an individualized
time, just to participate in ashram life of Aarti-puja,
asana, meditation, kirtan chanting, and karma yoga.
Karma Yoga is an opportunity to serve (and purify
the mind!) in a range of ways from cleaning to
gardening to chopping vegetables.

Courses are taught by Mataji and her three children,
Ganga, Mandakini, and Alaknanda, Acharyas in Yoga
and Ayurveda. Most programs will introduce you to
more than one teacher, and of course all are
available for conversations, "in the moment
teachings," - or a bath in the Ganga!

Courses include: The Bhagavad Gita, Patanjali's Yoga

Sutras, Ayurveda, Hatha Yoga and Meditation, and Clinical Yoga. (All classes are taught in English.)

Visit the website for a full list of courses, celebrations, dates, and more information! www.yoganga.org

The current Santosh Puri Ashram.

BOOK ORDERING INFORMATION

You may order copies of this book through the Printer's website **www.dogearsetc.com.** They will print and ship your order to anywhere in the world. (Their website includes a postal calculation table.)

Please contact Santosh Puri Ashram if you would like to distribute the book or to translate it into your language.

REFLECTIONS ON BABAJI:
REMEMBRANCES FROM DEVOTEES

One

Being in the presence of Baba Santosh Puriji was a Grace. My time with him became the root and foundation of my sadhana practice. The very early hours of the morning sitting by the duni in meditation with Babaji and Mataji, Narmada Puri, were precious.

Being in his presence during meditation, the veil of thoughts melted away like fog in the coming daylight. The sense of "I" melted into the pulsation of the present moment. This was the nature of Babaji's being and the essence of "What Is".

After experiencing this Grace, Babaji often just smiled or sent me off to do seva.
Always when I went off to work, his Grace continued flowing and surrounding me as if it had always been there, simply realized again by the Grace of the Guru - a lean fakir, a being of Truth, a yogi beyond words, beyond facades, a Self-realized soul. Realizing the Oneness of the non-dualistic consciousness of Being, of God, of Shiva.
Pranam Babaji, you truly manifest Om Namah Shivaya.

Everyone was welcome at Babaji's duni. People of all religions, races, castes and creeds came to be in his presence; Sadhus from different Akharas and orders, high-ranked Pandits sitting next to low or out-caste workers, criminals beside policemen and merchants, Western searchers of Truth and farmers from Hariyana, Muslims, Hindus and Christians, as well as our dogs and the cows. All enjoyed being near Babaji.

One time a Brahmin priest asked Babaji, "Why do you let all these strange people stay at your duni? You are a Hindu, a Sannyasin."
Babaji just smiled and said, "I am no Hindu, no Muslim, no Christian. I am a fakir, a yogi. I have no temple, the Ganga is my temple."
Babaji lived in this way. For him, all were the same. He lived in Atman consciousness. All is ONE.
A living example of Advaita.

Many times in the middle of the night I awoke to see Babaji sitting in meditation while everyone slept...and in the very early morning, he was the always the first to rise...blowing his conch, then singing aarti, tapping his knees with both hands in the joyful rhythm of the Divine.

Babaji, a yogi, a devotee of Ganga Ma, an awakened being.
Pranam, Babaji.

Narayan Puri/Rolf Naujakot, Disciple of Babaji, Ashtanga Yoga Teacher, Goa, India
www.yogabones.org

Two

Babaji never taught me anything, no concepts were exchanged, he did not add to my considerable intellectual baggage by giving me more ideas and notions about Truth. He was a Master in whose presence flowers came to bloom and blossom. It was by his very being that people who came to him received benefit.

Babaji was not one of those who had overly religious airs. He was a free spirit and celebrated the existence and humanity of all. A nod or a smile from Babaji was as empowering as any speech or teaching.

And for those who never had his darshan and wonder who he really was and why those that knew him loved him so much, all you have to do is go to Sri Santosh Puri Ashram and sit for a while in his Samadhi Garden and you will feel the subtle force of his divine presence aligning you to your breath, consciousness, hope and liberation.

Tim Williams, Devotee, United Kingdom

Published by Santosh Puri Ashram

www.yoganga.org

January 2009

Printing & distribution by Cinnamonteal Print and Publishing

Order copies of this book at: www.dogearsetc.com